Homestyle
CHINESE
Cooking

Homestyle CHINESE Cooking

By

YAN-KIT SO

THE CROSSING PRESS
FREEDOM, CALIFORNIA

For information on bulk purchases or group discounts for this and other Crossing Press titles, please contact our Special Sales Manager at 800-777-1048.

Visit our Web site on the Internet at: www.crossingpress.com

Library of Congress Cataloging-in-Publication Data

So, Yan-kit.
    Homestyle Chinese cooking / by Yan-kit So.
        p. cm. – (Homestyle cooking)
    Includes index.
    ISBN 0-89594-883-4 (paper)
    1. Cookery, Chinese. 2. Wok cookery. I. Title. II. Series.
TX724.5.C5S623 1997
641.5951–dc21   97-24538
                                                                         CIP

Acknowledgments

I am indebted to Professor Joseph Needham for pointing me in the right direction in my research into the history of the work, a subject that has been little explored. Thanks are also due to Mrs. Man-tong Yip for sending me research material from Hong Kong. I also wish to thank Chef Woo Kwun of Fung Shing Restaurant in Soho for inspiring several recipes, notably Stir-Fried Scallops, Phoenix Rolls, and Smoked Halibut. Last, but not least, I would like to thank my editor, Gill Cormode, whose sustaining interest not only in tasting my food but also in trying out some of the recipes herself made the writing and cooking of them that much more fun.

To my Mother and to Lady Brunner

CONTENTS

PREFACE

Of all the many different kinds of Chinese dishes, if not all the foods in the world, I confess that my favorites are those stir-fried in the wok. Such dishes are light, juicy, healthy and, above all, so fragrant that I can never tire of them. It is not surprising, therefore, that in my pursuit of the Chinese culinary art as a cook, teacher, demonstrator, and writer, I aspire to make stir-frying my forté, like so many great Chinese chefs. The chopping and cutting up of ingredients is, admittedly, time-consuming and patience-trying, but I accept it as a worthwhile necessity. When it comes to marinating, an essential part of Chinese cooking, I enjoy the mixing of flavors, seemingly at random but really aimed at achieving either a well-balanced result or an emphasis on a particular flavor.

You may well ask why in this book the measurements for the seasonings are so exact, down to the last 1/4 or 1/8 of a teaspoon! Do the Chinese really cook this way? The answer is no. Like all good cooks, they instinctively sprinkle in a pinch of salt, a dash of soy, a bit of sugar, and a splash of wine. And yet, if you actually watch them do so, you will note the "pinch" and the "bit" always measure more or less the same. For those new to Chinese cooking who are not familiar with the simple art of mixing those flavors so essential to the success of Chinese cooking, I have painstakingly worked out the balanced amount for them. But by all means free yourself from my guidelines and start having fun mixing your own concoctions of flavors. Only by doing so will you become your own expert Chinese cook!

What captures my imagination about stir-frying is the very operation itself—exhilarating, verging on a sense of theater. I love the near-explosive sound of the sizzling of the garlic and scallion and the splashing of the wine. When I wield the wok scoop and turn and toss the morsels around in the wok, I feel as if I were a conjurer, magically, in the twinkling of an eye, changing the raw pieces into a succulent and fragrant dish.

For me, there is nothing more therapeutic than stirring away in the wok to get rid of any pent-up emotion or tension I may feel, nor is there anything more gratifying than to have a wokful of goodies shared and enjoyed by my family and friends.

Rice is the staple food for the Chinese on a national basis, although noodles and steamed breads and buns are just as important a staple food for people in northern China. All Chinese dishes are eaten with rice—plain, boiled white rice as a rule. But, by all means, serve some of the dishes in this book with noodles, spaghetti, potatoes, or whatever staple food takes your fancy.

Unless otherwise stated, every dish in this book yields about six helpings. The Chinese always share the dishes, which are put on the table together. Even a piece of fish, such as a fish steak, would be broken up with chopsticks and everyone would help themselves. For an everyday meal I would suggest making two, and at the most three, dishes to serve four people.

THE WOK

The last three decades saw such an increased interest all over the world in Chinese cooking that in the late 1970s "wok" appeared in the *Collins English Dictionary*. Wok is the Cantonese pronunciation, while *guo* is the *pinyin* Chinese. But in China today, as in the rest of the world, this thin-walled, hemispherical pan, made more often than not of carbon iron than of cast iron, is known as the wok.

The wok's virtues cannot be extolled in sufficient superlatives. It is the most economical and versatile cooking utensil in the world, and its efficacy is difficult to exaggerate. Its wall, as thin as a metal sheet, makes for the quickest transmission of heat, resulting in the best economy in fuel consumption and the shortest duration of cooking time. In this one utensil, the whole spectrum of Chinese cooking techniques—stir-frying, sautéing, deep-frying, boiling, steaming, and even braising, to name but the major ones—can be executed. When called upon to perform beyond its Chinese duties, like tossing spaghetti with carbonara sauce or frying Chicken Kiev, it does equally well. So well established is its universal usage in the 1990s that it is not a question of listing which country under the umbrella of the United Nations uses the wok, but rather one of asking which country does not. So popular has it become, especially among the young and health conscious, that department stores vie with each other at Christmas time to sell the largest number of gift wok sets, complete with dome covers, rings, scoops and sometimes even brushes and chopsticks.

Archaeological evidence shows that the wok traces its origin to before the Christian era. But it is not easy to chronicle its evolution from its most ancient to its present form. This, no doubt, is partly due to the fact that iron rusts away, and many an ancient wok did not survive. Also, because it was a utilitarian vessel rather than a precious object, it was used much less by the nobility as a burial artifact. The story that has emerged, gleaned from archaeological finds, is fascinating, but still leaves intriguing questions unanswered.

The Iron Age began in Greece about 1200 bc, but it did not begin in China until 500–600 bc, although some authorities would say it started earlier. What is remarkable is that almost as soon as iron was known to the Chinese, they discovered the technology of melting and casting it. So by the 4th century bc, China was already producing cast iron. Agricultural tools were made and, during the Han dynasty (206 bc to ad 220), cast-iron pots, the ancestors of the wok, came into existence. It is worth mentioning that cast iron was not produced in Europe until the late 14th century, and then only in small quantities. Large-scale production did not follow until very early in the 18th century, and the first things made from cast iron were probably cooking vessels.

From the limited number of excavated specimens that have been written about in Chinese archaeological journals, two types of cast-iron cooking pot with distinguishing features have been isolated. These are the *fu* (cauldron or pot) and the *guo* (pan or wok). The majority, the *fu*, are about 8 inches high with a round or flat bottom, a curving globular body narrowing upward toward the neck and lip. They may or may not have two looped handles, one on each side of the pot just above the belly.(1) That these iron pots were used for cooking, there is little doubt. Some excavated from a Later Han tomb (AD 25–220) still show burn marks and have soot on the outside; at least one was found sitting on a three-legged iron stand,(2) and another holding a clay pot or *zeng* on top for steaming food(3) (see facing page). It is difficult to ascertain how widely used they were, especially among the common people. The most basic cooking utensil at that time was made of earthenware, for both the rich and the poor, while bronze ware was also in use.

The other type of pot, the *guo*, has a round bottom and is hemispherical in shape, with an open and wide rim and two handles. One *guo*, even though it is very small, measuring 3 1/3 inches in depth and 5 1/2 inches across the rim, and with one loop handle missing, looks remarkably like the present-day wok, although it is too deep in proportion to its width across the rim.(4) What is very interesting, though, is that another *guo*, much larger and thicker, was in fact used to smelt bronze for coining money.

During the next six centuries after the Han dynasty, there does not seem to be any excavated specimen to chart the development of the cast-iron cooking pot.

The next group of specimens, excavated near Peking and in northeast China, notably from historical sites rather than from tombs, date from the 10th to the 14th centuries. The majority are known as six-handled pots, so called because of the six flat, rectangular handles attached at regular intervals around the exterior wall of the pot. Circular and with a round

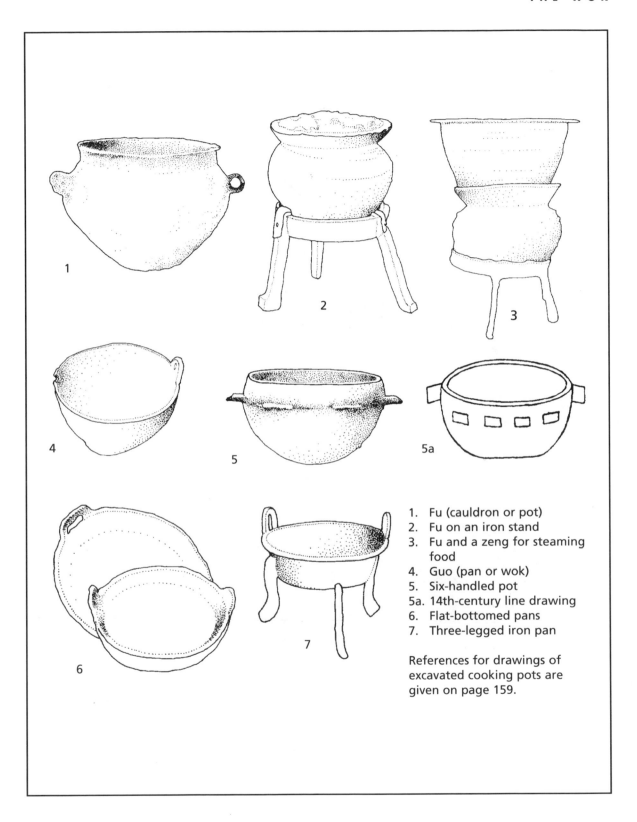

1. Fu (cauldron or pot)
2. Fu on an iron stand
3. Fu and a zeng for steaming food
4. Guo (pan or wok)
5. Six-handled pot
5a. 14th-century line drawing
6. Flat-bottomed pans
7. Three-legged iron pan

References for drawings of excavated cooking pots are given on page 159.

bottom, the pot is deep, but is even wider across the rim, which sometimes rolls slightly outward. The largest one, found in northeast China, is 12 1/2 inches high, 20 inches across the rim and 26 1/3 inches across the widest part of the body just where the handles are.(5) These pots were used by rural communities for cooking noodles. In the famous 14th-century book, *Work on Agriculture* (Nong Shu), there is a line drawing of the six-handled pot,(5a) which, except for its flat bottom, looks very similar to the excavated specimen.

A parallel development to the six-handled pot is manifest in the doubled-handle pan, a pair of which were excavated in 1969 near Peking in the same site as the six-handled pot. Both flat-bottomed with soot and burn marks still apparent on the exterior, the pans measure 2 1/4 inches and 2 1/2 inches in height against a rim diameter of 15 1/2 inches and 12 inches respectively. Notably, the iron pans have two handles on opposite sides of the rim, not unlike the present-day wok handles.(6)

Another type of iron pan of the same period is the three-legged pan, shallow, flat-bottomed, having two handles on opposite sides and three legs attached to the base.(7) Obviously, the function of the legs was to allow fuel to be burned underneath the pan.

Both the double-handled and the three-legged pans were probably used for sautéing and for frying cakes, as both their flat bottoms and shallow bodies are conducive to such cooking techniques.

When did the transformation to the present-day wok take place? This question is easier to ask than to answer. One literary reference, reinforced by a charming and convincing illustration of the actual casting of woks on molds, sheds much light on the subject. In *The Exploitation of the Works of Nature* (*Tian Gong Kai Wu*) published in 1637, there is a description and a drawing of the manufacturing of cast-iron woks *en masse*, not only in China but also in neighboring Korea. The size varied, the largest reputedly having a capacity to cook 2 piculs (or more than 250 pounds) of rice, enough to feed 1,000 monks! The measurements of the two standard-sized woks are given as follows: the larger had a rim diameter of about 28 inches and the smaller 14 inches, both about 1/3 inch thick. Our modern woks, in comparison, are thinner and lighter. What is so remarkable is that the smaller 14-inch wok is precisely what I use every day and have always recommended as the ideal size for home cooking.

The Wok Set

The multi-purpose lightweight wok, nowadays make of carbon iron, has a round bottom and either two metal or wooden handles or one long wooden handle. It fits over a brazier or a brick stove with fire holes, as is found in many homes in China.

To adapt the wok to the standard Western kitchen, it is advisable to acquire a wok set, complete with a lid or cover, a ring or stand, and a scoop.

The lid, usually made of aluminum with a wooden knob on top, is sometimes shaped like a round dome and sometimes a plateau dome. The latter, more spacious inside, is preferable, for it covers snugly a whole duck or chicken or a whole fish.

The stand, also metal, often has round holes around it, giving air to the gas flame. For deep-frying, steaming, braising, and making soups, when there is a large amount of boiling liquid or hot oil in the wok, it is essential that it sits securely on the stand. But for stir-frying and even sautéing, when the wok can be steadied by one mittened hand, the cooking is done more effectively without the stand.

The scoop, sometimes iron and sometimes stainless steel, looks like a shovel—indeed, such is the Chinese name for it—and it has a long handle with a wooden end for easy holding. Even though it is adequate to use a metal spatula, the wok scoop is constructed at such an angle as to facilitate the turning and tossing motion around the curved sides of the wok.

Personally, I have always preferred round-bottomed woks with two metal or wooden handles, and I have always used gas in my kitchen. Woks come in different sizes, but the 14-inch size is what I use and would recommend for home cooking, for it is both wide enough and deep enough in which to perform all the wok cooking techniques.

An iron wok with sloping sides and a small flat bottom (about 4 inches across) is available for people who cook with electricity. Needless to say, the flat-bottomed wok makes better contact with an electric coil than its round-bottomed counterpart. There are also electric woks that have their own element and a sensitive control knob, and I am told that they produce a satisfactory result. However, you should stay away from woks made of any metal other than iron, such as aluminum, copper, or stainless steel, because they are either too heavy or don't transmit heat as effectively.

Preparing and Caring for the Wok

A new wok often has a protective film of grease over it, which must be removed before use. To do so, fill the wok with water, add some detergent and boil the water for about half an hour, then throw it out. Next scrub the wok hard with an abrasive to rid it of the grease. Now rinse it and dry it over a low heat for about 5 minutes. When it is cool enough to handle, wipe both sides thoroughly with vegetable oil, using either a cloth or paper towel. The wok is now ready for cooking.

To clean the wok after each use, wash it with water, using a *mild* detergent if necessary, and a cloth or a soft brush. Do not scrub hard, otherwise you will scratch the surface. Dry thoroughly either over a low heat or with a cloth or paper towel and wipe all over again with a small amount of oil. The wok, being iron, rusts easily. The only remedy is to scrub off the rust and wipe over with oil. After a wok has been in constant use for a few months, it becomes well-seasoned, with a dark patina on the surface, and it rusts less easily as long as you keep it dry.

SPECIAL INGREDIENTS

Bamboo shoots

Young shoots from the bamboo are cultivated in China for the table. Fresh bamboo shoots are unfortunately seldom, if ever, available in the West, so that we have no option but to use the canned product. The shoots give a contrast of texture to other ingredients.

Chinese egg noodles

Sold in two forms, fresh or dried, Chinese egg noodles are made of wheat flour, egg, and water. Compared with Western noodles, they are more elastic in texture. If they are not available, use noodles from other countries as a substitute.

Cloud ears

Edible tree fungi are cultivated in large quantities in western China. Sold dried, they are black in color and brittle to the touch. When reconstituted (see page 25), they are used as an absorber of tastes and they lend a slimy, yet crunchy, texture to other ingredients.

Dried Chinese black mushrooms

Black in appearance, these are specially cultivated tree fungi used as an accompanying ingredient and sometimes as a main ingredient. They lend taste to other ingredients and absorb other tastes, which in turn makes them even more succulent. The Japanese cultivate and supply them to Chinese and Western markets, so they are also well known by the Japanese name, *shiitake*. They have to be reconstituted before use (see page 25)

Dried shrimp

Orangey pink in color, their saltiness mitigated by a savory sweet overtone, and varying in sizes, they are used as a seasoning for vegetables and soups and in stuffings.

Fermented black beans

These are whole soybeans fermented and preserved in salt and ginger; the dried ones are better than those canned in brine. When combined with garlic and cooked in oil, they become the famous black bean sauce used for a whole range of Chinese dishes.

Five-spice powder

A finely ground golden brown powder made up of five or six spices including star anise, cinnamon, fennel, cloves, and Sichuan peppercorns. Used in marinades, it must be used sparingly, otherwise it will impart an unpleasant taste to the main ingredient.

Fresh bean curd

Ivory white curd made from ground soy beans and sold in cakes varying in size. Very healthy and nutritious, it is one of the most versatile ingredients in Chinese cooking. It is also known by its Japanese name, *tofu*.

Golden needles

This euphemistic name is in reality the term for dried, unopened tiger-lily flowers measuring about 3 inches in length and looking golden brown in color. When reconstituted (see page 25), they are used to provide a subtle lightness of texture while they themselves absorb tastes from other ingredients.

Hoisin sauce

Lusciously dark brown, made from soy beans, salt, wheat flour, sugar, vinegar, garlic, chili and sesame oil resulting in a savory sweet but tangy taste, it is used both as a seasoning or as a dipping sauce for meats, such as roast pork and roast duck. It comes in either bottles or cans.

Oil

The Chinese normally use peanut oil, but they also use corn oil and vegetable oil.

Oyster sauce

A special southern Chinese sauce made from extracts of oysters, it is nut brown, usually bottled but sometimes also canned. Less strong than soy sauce but more expensive, its special value lies in the sweet and "meaty" taste it lends to other ingredients, whether meat, vegetables, rice, or noodles. It is used as a dipping sauce or as a finishing touch to a sauce mixture.

Pickled salty and sour plums

These come in a jar and can be bought at your nearest Chinese store.

Raw frozen shrimp

Shrimp dishes are an important feature in the Chinese cuisine, and they are always prepared from their raw state, just as meat and fish dishes are. Shrimp that are already boiled are not suitable for Chinese cooking. Fortunately, frozen raw shrimp are available in Chinese and Oriental stores as well as at most supermarkets, and I would strongly advise trying to get them.

Rice vinegar

Clear and mild vinegar made from rice. White wine vinegar can act as a substitute.

Shaoxing wine

Amber-colored Chinese wine made from glutinous rice, used both for drinking and for cooking. For drinking, it tastes much better slightly warmed; for cooking, a medium-dry sherry can be used as a good substitute.

Sichuan peppercorns

Otherwise known as *fagara*, these small, reddish brown peppercorns are a special product of Sichuan province in western China. Not as burning hot as black peppercorns, they produce a slight numbing effect made more enticing by their aroma. They are used in stews and braised dishes.

Soy sauce

Made from fermented, protein-rich soy beans, this is an indispensable seasoning to Chinese cooking. There are two main kinds, the thick and the thin, or the dark and the light, both of which are used in Chinese homes and restaurants. Thick soy sauce is darker in color, thicker in consistency and less salty in taste, while thin soy sauce is lighter, thinner, and more salty. Often they are used together in conjunction with salt, but since thick soy sauce gives a reddish-brown hue to food, do not use it in marinating or seasoning ingredients when a light appearance is called for. Soy sauce is usually packaged in bottles but also comes in cans.

Star anise

The French use anise seeds in their cooking, but the Chinese use the whole, eight-segmented, hard spice with its licorice taste to flavor their stews and braised dishes. Reddish brown in color, it does resemble a star, hence its name.

Thickening agents

In Chinese cooking, a range of thickening agents are used: arrowroot, tapioca flour, water chestnut flour, potato starch and cornstarch, but the last two are more common and easily available. Compared to cornstarch, potato starch is more gelatinous and gives a more subtle and glossy finish to a sauce, but because it is more gelatinous, the quantity used must be less than for the cornstarch.

Wonton skins

Thin as skin and usually about 3 inches square, these wonton wrappers are made of wheat, egg and water. Sold fresh in plastic bags in Chinese stores, they can be frozen.

SPECIAL TECHNIQUES

TO MAKE SPICED SALT

Many Chinese dishes, such as Lemon Chicken (page 116) and Crispy Skin Bean Curd (page 144) benefit from being dipped in a little spiced salt. It enhances the flavor of the food.

To prepare the spiced salt, heat the wok over a medium heat until hot, but not smoking. Add 2 tablespoons salt and stir continuously for 4–5 minutes, or until very hot and slightly grayish in color. Remove to a small bowl, add 1 tablespoon five-spice powder and 1/2 teaspoon ground white or black pepper. Mix well and serve in small saucers at the table.

TO MAKE GINGER JUICE

While the Chinese adore fish, they abhor the fishy odor and believe that ginger counters this odor most effectively.

To prepare ginger juice, peel a large chunk of fresh ginger, mince it finely or grate it, and then squeeze out the juice with your hand into a container. Discard the pulp. The juice keeps for a long time if refrigerated.

To make a small amount, see Chinese Broccoli with Ginger Juice, page 97, step 3.

TO RECONSTITUTE A DRIED INGREDIENT

Dried products, such as Chinese black mushrooms, cloud ears, and golden needles, have to be reconstituted in order to return them to their former pliable state. To do this, soak them for 20 minutes or longer in enough hot water for them to expand fully. Then remove them from the soaking liquid, squeeze out excess water, but leave them damp. The soaking liquid for the black mushrooms can be reserved for the stockpot or for sauce, but the liquid for cloud ears and golden needles should be discarded.

There is often fine sand or other impurities attached to cloud ears and it is therefore advisable to rub them gently once they have expanded in the soaking liquid, plucking off at the same time the hard knobs found on them. As for golden needles, simply chop off the small hard ends after removing them from the liquid.

SOUPS

▲▲▲▲▲▲▲▲▲▲▲▲▲▲▲

It may sound ridiculous to make soups in the wok, but the Chinese actually do, and with remarkable success. To be sure, they also use ordinary deep saucepans to make soups and sometimes they combine the use of both. For example, the stock may be made in a saucepan and then the soup made with some of the stock in a wok.

Unlike a Western soup, which is often quite thick and cream-based, a Chinese soup is basically a thin, clear broth, with or without some ingredients swimming in it. The most commonly used ingredients are vegetables, either chopped up or sliced, sometimes seasoned with small pieces of meat or fish. For instance, a Chinese cook may use meaty spareribs as a base and add a few Chinese mushrooms. In the old days, the cook would have added a little bit "from the sea," such as the dried *abalone*, which is now so expensive that it is out of the reach of most people's pockets. Water would be added, and the soup simmered for a couple of hours. If a soup is not tasty enough, it is sprinkled with a little (1 or 2 teaspoons) of the magical soy sauce.

The Chinese love to have a bowl of soup with every meal. In the Western sequence of serving a meal, the soup always precedes the main course. In the Chinese sequence, a bowl of clear broth may be put side by side with a bowl of rice for day-to-day family fare. An exotic soup, such as the classic shark's fin or bird's nest, may come several courses down the line in a banquet. Then again, there may be another soup, the clear broth kind, a few dishes after the exotic soup.

In the Chinese home, you would never see many of the soups served in Chinese restaurants abroad, such as the immensely popular wonton soup. The Chinese would consider wonton (which are rather similar to pork ravioli) as dumplings in a broth, to be eaten for lunch or as a snack.

Mussels in Soup

The wok, with its wide hemispherical shape, is most conducive to cooking mussels, for it allows plenty of room for the mussels to cook and open quickly, and thus stay very juicy. If you like the taste of ginger at all, you will find the accompanying soup, marked by a subtle ginger and wine flavor, agreeable indeed.

INGREDIENTS

2 1/2–3 pounds mussels
4 tablespoons vegetable oil
2–3 garlic cloves, roughly chopped
1 1/2–2 inches fresh ginger, sliced, peeled, and well bruised
2 shallots, roughly chopped
1 large onion, roughly chopped
1 cup white wine (preferably Sauternes) or cider
1/4 teaspoon salt, or to taste
White pepper to taste
Small bunch cilantro leaves for garnish, trimmed

METHOD

■ Scrub and wash the mussels thoroughly, one by one, until they are very clean. Pull off the "beards" between the shells and knock off the barnacles with the back of a knife. Discard any mussels that are broken or remain open when you tap them. Put in a colander to drain.

■ Heat the wok over a high heat until smoke rises. Add the oil and swirl it around several times. Add the garlic, let sizzle and take on color, then add the ginger and stir until its aroma is released. Add the shallots and stir for a few more seconds. Lower the heat and add the onion. Stir and cook for about 5 minutes, or until the onion is soft. Turn up the heat again, pour in the wine or cider, bring to a fast boil, and reduce it by about one-fourth. Season with the salt and pepper.

■ Place the wok on its stand to make it more steady. Pour in the mussels. Sliding the wok scoop or a spatula to the bottom of the wok, give several sweeping turns. Cover with the wok lid and continue to cook over a moderately high heat for about 4 minutes, or until the mussels are wide open, indicating that they are cooked. Discard those that remain closed.

■ Remove the wok from the heat. Scoop the mussels and the accompanying soup into a large soup tureen. Arrange the cilantro leaves on top and serve immediately.

Beef Meatball Soup

A soup sufficiently filling and nourishing to be served as lunch for four people. Although Chinese to the core, it will go very well with French bread. Try it.

INGREDIENTS

8 ounces ground beef
6 1/4 cups lightly seasoned beef or chicken stock
2 tablespoons vegetable oil
6 ounces fresh mushrooms, trimmed and cut into thin slices
2–3 scallions, green parts only, cut into tiny rounds
Salt and pepper to taste
MARINADE
1/4 teaspoon salt
Small pinch sugar
1 teaspoon thin soy sauce
2 teaspoons thick soy sauce
8–20 turns black pepper mill
1–1 1/2 teaspoons minced fresh ginger root
2 teaspoons Shaoxing wine or medium-dry sherry
2 teaspoons cornstarch
5–6 tablespoons water
1 teaspoon sesame oil
1 tablespoon vegetable oil

METHOD

■ Marinate the beef. Put the beef in a large mixing bowl. Add the salt, sugar, soy sauces, pepper, ginger, and wine or sherry and stir to mix. Sprinkle with the flour, then add the water, 1 tablespoon at a time, and stir vigorously in the same direction until completely absorbed before adding another spoonful. Pick up the whole lump of beef and throw it back into the bowl 50–60 times. This makes the beef light and slippery in texture. Leave in the refrigerator for 30 minutes or longer. Blend in the oils.

■ With your fingers, pick up the 2–3 teaspoons of the meat and roll it into a ball about the size of a Ping-Pong ball. Repeat with all the beef.

■ Pour the stock into the wok and bring it to a boil. Add the oil. Add the mushrooms and cook over a gentle heat for 4–5 minutes. Add the meatballs. Return the soup to a fast simmer, then continue to cook for about 1 1/2 minutes, if you like the beef balls to be pink in the center, or 2 minutes longer, if you like them to be well done, stirring them around a couple of times. Add the scallions, give the soup another big stir, then remove from the heat.

■ Taste the soup for seasoning. Ladle the meatballs and soup either into a large soup tureen or into individual bowls. Serve hot.

West Lake Beef Soup

This soup purports to celebrate the picturesque and most famous lake in China, the West Lake, not too far away from Shanghai. To be absolutely correct, a small amount of only the leaves of watercress should float on the soup's misty surface, which is caused by the use of egg white. But I have used the stalk of the watercress as well because I don't see any point in wasting such a precious and delicious vegetable. If there is no watercress, just use some individual leaves of cilantro, good for decoration and taste.

INGREDIENTS

6 ounces beef, rump or fillet, trimmed and cut across the grain into rectangular slices about 1/2 x 1 1/4 inches and 1/4 inch thick

4 cups unseasoned chicken stock

1/4 teaspoon salt, or to taste

2 tablespoons vegetable oil

1 bunch, about 4 ounces, watercress, trimmed, washed, and well drained

MARINADE

1/2 teaspoon salt

1/2 teaspoon sugar

2 teaspoons thin soy sauce

6–8 turns white pepper mill

1 1/2 teaspoons Shaoxing wine or medium-dry sherry

2 teaspoons cornstarch

1 tablespoon water

1 small egg white

1 teaspoon sesame oil

1 tablespoon vegetable oil

METHOD

■ Marinate the beef. Add the salt, sugar, soy sauce, pepper, wine or sherry, and cornstarch to the beef and stir in the same direction to coat. Add the water and stir again until absorbed. Add the egg white, stirring again. Leave to stand in the refrigerator for 15–30 minutes. Blend in the oils.

■ Pour the stock into the wok and bring to a simmer. Add the salt and the oil. Add the beef, stir vigorously a couple of times with a pair of bamboo chopsticks or a wooden spoon, and return to a simmer. Remove at once from the heat. The beef will be still slightly underdone in the center and very tender. Submerge the watercress in the soup. Ladle either into a large soup tureen or individual soup bowls. Serve immediately.

Soup with Noodles and Shredded Pork

Noodles in a clear stock, topped by some meat or seafood and a few leafy vegetables, are eaten as a light meal from morning to night by many Chinese. It is served as frequently in noodle shops and street stalls as it is at home. You can vary the ingredients, using chicken, beef, shrimp or crabmeat, and other vegetables.

INGREDIENTS

12 ounces lean pork, cut into matchstick-size strips
12 ounces dried, or 1 pound fresh, Chinese egg noodles
6 1/4 cups lightly seasoned chicken stock
5 tablespoons vegetable oil
3 scallions, trimmed and cut into 1-inch sections, white and green parts separated
4–6 large iceberg or cos lettuce leaves, torn into pieces
Black or white pepper
Thin or thick soy sauce

MARINADE

1/2 teaspoon salt
1/4 teaspoon sugar
1 tablespoon thin soy sauce
6 turns white pepper mill
1 teaspoon Shaoxing wine or medium-dry sherry
1 1/2 teaspoons cornstarch
1 tablespoon water
1 teaspoon sesame oil

METHOD

■ Marinate the pork. Add the salt, sugar, soy sauce, pepper, wine or sherry, cornstarch, and water to the pork and stir to mix well. Leave to stand for 15–20 minutes, then blend in the oil.

■ Fill the wok with about 3 quarts of water and bring to a boil. Add the noodles and return to a boil. Using a pair of chopsticks or a fork, separate the noodles and continue to boil until *al dente*. Fresh noodles take about 1 1/2 minutes, dry ones 3–4 minutes, or longer. (Check the package for instructions.) Pour into a colander to drain. Divide the noodles into 6 portions. Put 1 portion into each of 4 individual bowls, and the remaining 2 portions into a large serving bowl for second helpings.

■ Add the stock to the wok and bring to a gentle boil. Add 3 tablespoons of the oil and the white scallions. Add the pork, separate with chopsticks or fork, and simmer for 45–60 seconds, or until opaque. Using a perforated spoon, lift about one-sixth of the pork and scallions each time and place on the noodles in the 4 bowls. Add the remainder to the large bowl.

■ Return the soup to a boil and add the remaining 2 tablespoons oil. Add the lettuce and the green scallions, return to a gentle boil, then remove the wok from the heat. Divide the lettuce and scallions as before.

■ Divide the soup among the individual bowls and the large bowl and serve immediately. Pepper and soy sauce can be used at the table to individual taste.

Shredded Pork Soup

The fresh mushrooms add a sweetness to the chicken-based stock, while the cilantro leaves lend an overall fragrance to the soup. Even so, to make the soup truly delicious, the pork slices must be tender and not overcooked. An even simpler way to make this soup is to use shredded ham. Obviously, with ham there is no need to marinate the meat. If you want to make a more substantial soup, you could add a handful of Chinese noodles or small Italian pasta shapes.

INGREDIENTS

4 ounces trimmed lean pork, cut into rectangular slices about 1/2 x 1 1/2 inches and 1/8 inch thick

4 1/2–5 cups unseasoned chicken stock

1 1/2 tablespoons vegetable oil

1/4–1/2 teaspoon salt, or to taste

4 ounces fresh mushrooms, trimmed and cut into thin slices

4 stalks cilantro leaves (branches of leaves only)

MARINADE

1/4–1/2 teaspoon salt

2 teaspoons thin soy sauce

4 turns white pepper mill

1 teaspoon Shaoxing wine or medium-dry sherry

1 teaspoon cornstarch

1/2 tablespoon water

1 teaspoon sesame oil

1 teaspoon vegetable oil

METHOD

■ Marinate the pork. Add the salt, soy sauce, pepper, wine or sherry, and cornstarch to the pork and stir to coat. Add the water and stir again until well absorbed. Leave to stand for 15–20 minutes. Blend in the oils.

■ Pour the stock into the wok and bring it to a gentle boil. Add the oil and the salt. Add the mushrooms and continue to cook for 4–5 minutes, maintaining a gentle boil.

■ Add the pork, separate the pieces with chopsticks or a fork and return to a gentle boil, continuing to cook for another minute, or until the pork is just cooked, having turned opaque. Remove the wok from the heat. Check the soup for seasoning. Immerse the cilantro leaves into the soup before spooning into either a large soup tureen or individual bowls. Serve immediately.

STEAMING

▲▲▲▲▲▲▲▲▲▲▲▲▲▲▲▲▲▲▲

What's so special about the Chinese method of steaming is that all the goodness and taste of the ingredients are retained, whereas one associates Western steaming with tastelessness. The method of steaming is as follows: Place the wok on its stand on top of the burner. Put either a metal trivet or a small bamboo cage upside down in the center of the wok. Put whatever food is to be steamed on a shallow heatproof dish, so that the juices are retained in the dish when the food is cooked. Put the dish on the metal or bamboo stand. Next, fill the wok with boiling water to about 1 inch of the base of the dish in order to prevent the bubbling water from getting into the dish and spoiling the food. Place the lid on the wok and turn up the heat, maintaining it at the same intensity to ensure that plenty of steam rises from the boiling water and circulates inside the covered wok to cook the food. If the food is to be steamed for a long time, as is the case for a duck, be sure to replenish the water from time to time. A piece of fish, however, cooks through very quickly. Another small but important point to bear in mind is this: Refrain from lifting the wok lid unnecessarily, for every time you do so, steam escapes and you will need to steam the food for a longer period in order to make sure it is cooked.

Steaming is one of the oldest cooking techniques in China, dating back at least 4,000 years. It was done in a primitive yet, for its time, most sophisticated steamer made of pottery or bronze. The base, called the *li*, was a cooking pot with three breast-shaped hollow legs that sat over a fire and in which water could be boiled or rice cooked. On top of the *li* stood a vessel called a *zeng*, which had a perforated flat bottom, the design of which is hardly changed today, through which steam came up to cook the food inside. This principle of steaming food has always remained the same, while the wok has long since become a substitute for the *li*.

Steamed Siu Mai

One of the most basic Cantonese *dim sum* (hors d'oeuvres) is *siu mai*, open-topped pork dumplings. It is worth your trouble and expense to get the raw shrimp rather than use just pork, as so many restaurants seem to do these days.

INGREDIENTS

1 pound shelled and deveined small raw shrimp, pat dried and coarsely minced
1 1/4 teaspoons salt
1 pound trimmed lean pork, finely minced
10 medium-sized dried Chinese mushrooms, reconstituted (see page 25) and finely minced
2 tablespoons thin soy sauce
1 1/4 teaspoons sugar
10 turns white pepper mill
2 tablespoons vegetable oil
1–2 teaspoons sesame oil
50–60 pieces wonton skin, each about 3 inches square (see page 24)

METHOD

■ Prepare the stuffing. Put the minced shrimp into a large bowl. Add the salt and, using either a pair of chopsticks or a fork, stir vigorously in the same direction for about 2 minutes or until the shrimp has become gelatinous. Add the minced pork and Chinese mushrooms, then add the soy sauce, sugar, and pepper. Stir in the same direction again for another 2–3 minutes, until the mixture is gelatinous. Leave to stand for 15–20 minutes. Stir in the oils.

■ Wrap the sui mai. Clip off the 4 corner triangles of 1 piece of wonton skin, then place it between the fingertips and the palm of one hand. Put about 1 tablespoon of stuffing on the center of the skin. Close your hand, squeezing the skin gently into an upright pouch, the skin forming natural pleats around the stuffing. Using a small knife, smooth down the stuffing to level with the top of the skin pleats, and squeeze gently to form a neck and ensure the stuffing remains stuck to the skin throughout the steaming. Stand the "pouches" on a flat surface to give them a flat bottom. Repeat until the stuffing is used up.

■ Steam the sui mai. Space them out on either an oiled bamboo steaming cage or a heatproof dish placed on a trivet, and steam in the wok, covered, until cooked. In a bamboo cage, the steaming time is 5–6 minutes; while in a dish, the time is 7–8 minutes. Serve piping hot.

NOTE *Sui mai* can be prepared in advance and frozen either before or after steaming.

Steamed Fish

The Chinese hanker after steamed fish much as Westerners crave beef steaks. The choicer and fresher the fish, the more likely it will be steamed rather than cooked in any other way. Sea bass is superb for steaming, but rainbow trout, gray mullet, lemon sole, and haddock, or even cod steak are subtly delicious. The key is to steam it without overcooking it.

To steam a fish "clear," only ginger and scallions are used; otherwise, the most usual condiment is the versatile black beans spread on the fish and steamed with it. If a fish or fish steak is too long for the heatproof dish on which it is steamed, halve it and put the pieces side by side. When cooked, add this finishing touch: Pour over it a small amount of hot oil and add some soy sauce which, mixed with the natural juices from the fish, will make a flavorful sauce.

INGREDIENTS

1 gray mullet, about 2 pounds, cleaned (about 1 1/2 pounds after cleaning) but with the head left on; or about 1 1/4 pounds fish steak, halibut, turbot, or cod, 3/4–1 inch thick
1/2 inch fresh ginger, peeled and finely shredded
4 large scallions, trimmed and cut into 2-inch sections, then finely shredded, white and green parts separated
3–4 tablespoons vegetable oil
2 1/2 tablespoons thick soy sauce
White pepper to taste

METHOD

■ Rinse the fish and pat dry. Halve crosswise. Put the two pieces side by side on a heatproof dish with raised edges. Spread the ginger on top and put some in the cavity.

■ Place the dish on the trivet in the wok and steam, tightly covered, over a high heat for 8–10 minutes, or until the fish turns opaque, the flesh barely coming away from the main bone.

■ Remove the lid. If too much liquid formed by the steam is found on the dish around the fish, dab some off with paper towels. Spread the green, then the white scallions on the fish. (For those who like their scallions more cooked, they can replace the lid and steam for 30–60 seconds.)

■ Heat the oil in a small saucepan until smoke rises. Pour it on the scallions, dribbling it down slowly so that the sizzling oil partially cooks the scallions.

■ Pour the soy sauce over the fish and season with pepper to taste. Serve immediately.

Steamed Minced Pork

A typical family dish for everyday consumption. The addition of dried Chinese mushrooms and bamboo shoots or water chestnuts to the pork makes the texture particularly pleasing to the palate. When cooked, it looks like a large meat patty. What the Chinese do is use thin chopsticks and lift away one bite-sized chunk at a time. You may prefer to cut it into small pieces with a knife first.

INGREDIENTS

12 ounces ground pork

4–6 medium-sized dried Chinese mushrooms, reconstituted (see page 25) and minced

2–3 ounces canned bamboo shoots or 6–8 canned water chestnuts, minced

4 scallions, cut into small rounds, white and green parts separated

2 tablespoons vegetable oil

1–2 teaspoons sesame oil

MARINADE

1/2 teaspoon salt

1/2 teaspoon sugar

2 teaspoons thin soy sauce

8 turns white pepper mill

2 teaspoons Shaoxing wine or medium-dry sherry

1 1/2 teaspoons cornstarch

4 tablespoons chicken stock

METHOD

■ Marinate the pork. Add the salt, sugar, soy, pepper, and wine or sherry to the pork and mix well. Sprinkle with the cornstarch, add the stock, 1 tablespoon at a time, stirring in the same direction until completely absorbed before adding another spoonful. This makes the pork fluffy and light. Leave to stand for 15–20 minutes.

■ Add the Chinese mushrooms, bamboo shoots or water chestnut and white scallions to the pork and mix evenly. Stir in the vegetable oil and sesame oil.

■ Spread this mixture onto a round heatproof serving dish, 8–10 inches in diameter with slightly raised edges. Put the dish into the wok and steam , covered tightly, over a high heat for 8–10 minutes, or until the pork is cooked. There will be some juice on the pork. Lift the wok cover, sprinkle on the green scallions, put the cover on again, and steam for about 5 seconds. Remove the dish and serve immediately.

Steamed Beef with Bamboo Shoots

This family dish is so succulent that it is also fit for the most special of guests. Just like roast beef or steak, you can have it any way from well done to rare, depending on how you like it.

The bamboo shoots, which give a contrast of texture to the tender beef, can be replaced by a few mushrooms sliced very thinly.

Here I give one way of making ginger juice. The master recipe on page 25 is ideal for large quantities and for those who cook Chinese food all the time.

INGREDIENTS

12 ounces trimmed rump or skirt steak, cut into slices about 1 x 1 1/2 inches and 1/4 inch thick

4 ounces canned bamboo shoots, cut into thin slices

3–4 scallions, cut into 1-inch sections, white and green parts separated

1–2 tablespoons oil

MARINADE

1 inch fresh ginger, peeled and finely chopped

1/2 teaspoon salt

1/4 teaspoon sugar

1 1/2 tablespoons thick soy sauce

8 turns black pepper mill

2 teaspoons Shaoxing wine or medium-dry sherry

2 teaspoons cornstarch

1 tablespoon water

1 1/2 tablespoons vegetable oil

1 teaspoon sesame oil

METHOD

■ Marinate the beef. In 2–3 batches, put the ginger in a garlic press, add 2–3 drops of water each time and squeeze the resulting juice onto the beef, scraping in the minced ginger on the press as well, discarding the pulp inside. Add the salt, sugar, soy sauce, pepper, wine or sherry, and cornstarch and stir until well coated. Add the water and stir again. Leave to stand for 20–30 minutes. Blend in the oils.

■ Mix the bamboo shoots into the beef.

■ Spread the beef mixture over a heatproof dish with raised edges. Scatter the white scallions on top. Put the dish into the wok and steam, covered, for 4–5 minutes. The beef should be either just done or slightly underdone, depending on personal taste. Remove the wok cover, mix the beef to ensure the cornstarch is well cooked, then scatter on the green scallions. Steam, covered, for another 30–45 seconds. Remove the dish. Heat the oil in a small saucepan until smoke rises, and pour it onto the beef. Serve, preferably from the same dish.

Steamed Chicken Fillet

Steamed chicken is regular family fare for the Chinese. As often as not, the chicken is cut up into pieces through the skin and bones (see Variation), for the Chinese love to chew around the bones, believing that the meat around them is more succulent and tasty than white meat. Try both the recipe and the variation and judge for yourself. You may like it both ways.

INGREDIENTS

10–12 ounces chicken breast fillet without skin, cut into pieces about 1/2 inch wide

4–5 ounces fresh white mushrooms, trimmed and cut into 1/4-inch slices

4 thin slices fresh ginger, peeled

4–6 scallions, cut into 1-inch sections

MARINADE

1/2 teaspoon salt

1/2 teaspoon sugar

1 tablespoon thin soy sauce

6 turns white pepper mill

2 teaspoons Shaoxing wine or medium-dry sherry

2 teaspoons cornstarch

1 1/2 tablespoons egg white

2 1/2–3 tablespoons vegetable oil

1 teaspoon sesame oil

METHOD

■ Marinate the chicken in a bowl. Add the salt, sugar, soy sauce, pepper, wine or sherry, cornstarch, and egg white to the chicken and mix to coat evenly. Leave to stand for about 15 minutes. Stir in the oils. Add the mushrooms and mix with the chicken.

■ Transfer the mixture onto a heatproof plate with raised sides, spreading it out into a single layer, if possible. Scatter the ginger and scallions on top.

■ Steam in the wok for about 8 minutes, until the chicken is cooked, having turned white. There will be juice around the chicken from the steaming, which is delicious. Remove from the wok and serve, preferably straight from the same plate.

VARIATION: STEAMED DRUMSTICKS AND WINGS

Chop 3 drumsticks through the skin and bone with a cleaver into 3 pieces each. Joint 3 wings and halve each section. Proceed as above and steam the chicken for about 15 minutes, until cooked.

Steamed Duck with a Plum Sauce

This dish finds special favor with the Cantonese during the summer months, when it is very humid and hot in subtropical South China. The sweet-and-sour plum sauce reduces the grease of the duck and rouses people's appetite to eat even in the heat.

INGREDIENTS

1 4–4 1/2-pound oven-ready duck, oil sacs removed and discarded
1 teaspoon thick soy sauce
1 tablespoon vegetable oil
Vinegar to taste
1 1/2 tablespoons Shaoxing wine or medium-dry sherry
Several teaspoons cornstarch

PLUM SAUCE

6 ounces pickled salty and sour plums plus 1–2 tablespoons liquid from the jar
3–4 tablespoons sugar
1 teaspoon salt

METHOD

■ Prepare the plum sauce. Pit the plums (reserving the stones) and mash with the liquid. Add the sugar and salt.

■ Scald the duck by pouring a large kettle of boiling water over it. As the water is poured over the skin, it shrinks and becomes shiny. Wipe off any excess water. While the skin is still warm, brush all over with the soy sauce to add color.

■ Heat the wok over a high heat until smoke rises. Add the oil and swirl it around. Add the duck, breast side down, and brown for 45–60 seconds. Turn over to brown the back and then the sides in the same way. Remove and discard the oil. Wash the wok and set it up for steaming (see page 43).

■ Place the duck in a heatproof dish with raised sides. Spread the plum sauce and half of the pits over the skin; put the remaining pits inside the cavity. Steam for about 1 1/2 hours, until the duck is tender, replenishing the water in the wok 2–3 times.

■ Remove the duck to another dish and scrape the plum sauce into a saucepan. Discard the pits. Spoon off most of the fat on the liquid in the heatproof dish, then pour the liquid into the saucepan. Test for taste and add a little vinegar, and more salt and sugar, if necessary. Add the wine or sherry. Slowly bring to a simmer and thicken with cornstarch, allowing 1 teaspoon 1 1/2 teaspoons cornstarch dissolved in 1 tablespoon water for every 3 fluid ounces of sauce. Keep the sauce hot.

■ Either chop the duck through the bones into 1-inch pieces the Chinese way or carve it. Pour over the plum sauce and serve immediately.

STIR-FRYING

▲▲▲▲▲▲▲▲▲▲▲▲▲▲▲▲▲▲

As a technique in Chinese cooking, stir-frying came later than boiling, steaming, stewing, and roasting on a spit. Yet it is this ingenious technique that has captured the imagination of the whole world, so much so that many people regard it as synonymous with Chinese cuisine.

The technique consists of adding cut-up ingredients to an intensely heated wok containing a small amount of oil, then turning and tossing them around the curved sides until they are cooked just to a turn, with most of the vitamins still intact. This method can be used for cooking any foodstuff, be it vegetable, meat, seafood, rice, or noodles. Vegetables stir-fried are crisp and crunchy, meat and seafood are tender and juicy, but above all, they are impregnated down to the last morsel with a special fragrance the Chinese unashamedly term "wok fragrance."

How to achieve the best stir-fried results? A closer look at the process reveals the clues. The ingredients are always cut up into more or less uniform sizes so that they are cooked at the same time. Pieces of meat more often than not are marinated so that the mixed flavors, interacting with the oil and the condiments, permeate each morsel. The wok itself is always heated until it is red-hot before oil is poured in and swirled around. The oil is then seasoned by one or two if not all three of the basic condiments—ginger, garlic, and scallions—sometimes known as the Chinese family trinity in the kitchen. Speed, instant control of heat, and dexterous turning and tossing of the ingredients in the wok, if not actually tossing them in mid-air as so dramatically performed by the professional male Chinese chefs, are the next essential steps so that the ingredients can be cooked quickly without becoming tough or soggy. Although not absolutely necessary, the splashing in of a small amount of alcohol enhances the fragrance as the food sizzles in the wok. The addition of a simple sauce, usually soy sauce-based with a tiny amount of dissolved thickening, completes the operation. And we have a healthy, delicious, and fragrant dish to eat!

Shrimp in Black Bean Sauce

In preparing this dish, the goal is to make the texture of the shrimp crisp. Thus, both ginger and alcohol are to be avoided.

INGREDIENTS

1 pound medium-sized fresh or frozen raw shrimp in the shell, shelled and deveined
4 tablespoons vegetable oil
1 large green pepper, seeded and roughly chopped
4–5 garlic cloves, finely chopped
2 fresh red chiles, seeded and cut into small rounds (optional)
3 scallions, cut into 1-inch sections, white and green parts separated
2 tablespoons preserved black beans (see page 22), mashed with 1–2 teaspoons water and 1/2 teaspoon sugar
3/4 teaspoon cornstarch dissolved in 3 tablespoons water or chicken stock

MARINADE

1/2 teaspoon salt
1 teaspoon cornstarch
1 tablespoon egg white

METHOD

■ Marinate the shrimp. Pat the shrimp dry, then add the salt, cornstarch, and egg white and stir in the same direction to coat. Leave to stand, covered, in the refrigerator for 1–2 hours. (It can also be left overnight.) This process gives the shrimp the crisp texture looked for when cooked.

■ Heat the wok over a medium heat until hot. Add 1 tablespoon of the oil and swirl it around. Add the green pepper and stir for about 2 minutes. Remove to a dish and keep nearby. Wipe dry the wok.

■ Reheat over a high heat until smoke rises. Add the remaining 3 tablespoons oil and swirl it around several times. Add the garlic, let sizzle, then the chiles and white scallions and stir a few times. Add the mashed black beans, stirring to mix. Add the shrimp and, going to the bottom of the wok with the scoop or a metal spatula, turn and toss for 30–60 seconds, or until the shrimp are partially cooked, becoming pinkish. Lower the heat, pour in the well-stirred dissolved cornstarch, stirring as it thickens. Return the green pepper to the wok and add the green scallions, continuing to stir to mix. The shrimp should be fully cooked to a turn by now. Remove to a serving plate and serve immediately.

Stir-Fried Whole Scallops

Sea scallops are a luxurious treat. Their fibrous white meat, if not properly cooked, however, can become a rubbery mass, hateful to the palate. It is therefore worth your while to pay close attention to the timing given in this recipe if you wish to achieve the delicate and special dish it should be.

INGREDIENTS

1 1/2 pounds fresh sea scallops
1 1/2 teaspoons salt
2 tablespoons vegetable oil
4 ounces snow peas, trimmed
Oil for deep frying
2–3 garlic cloves, cut diagonally into slices
3–4 slices fresh ginger, peeled
2 scallions, cut into 2-inch sections, white and green parts separated
1 tablespoon Shaoxing wine or medium-dry sherry

SAUCE

1 1/2 teaspoons cornstarch
5–6 tablespoons well-seasoned ham or chicken stock

DIPS

Oyster sauce
Chili sauce

METHOD

■ Rinse the scallops and drain thoroughly. Slice each scallop in half horizontally.

■ Combine the sauce ingredients and set aside.

■ Half-fill the wok with boiling water, add 1 teaspoon of the salt and 1 tablespoon of the oil. Add the snow peas. As soon as the water returns to a fierce rolling boil, pour into a colander and quickly refresh the snow peas under cold running water. Drain thoroughly. This process retains the crispness and the vivid color of the snow peas, giving them a sheen as well. Dry the wok.

■ Fill the wok with about 3 cups oil and heat over a moderate heat to a temperature of 200–225° F, or until the oil is only moderately hot. Add the scallops and deep-fry for 1–1 1/2 minutes, separating any clumps with a long pair of chopsticks or wooden spoon. Lift the scallops with a large hand strainer or perforated spoon onto a dish.

■ Carefully empty all but about 1–2 tablespoons of the oil into a heatproof container and save for another use. Reheat the remaining oil until hot. Add the garlic, let sizzle and take on color, add the ginger and white scallions, and stir several times to release their aroma. Add the scallops, turn and toss with the wok scoop or metal spatula for 30 seconds. Season with 1/4 teaspoon salt. Splash the wine or sherry around the side of the wok, continuing to turn and toss until the sizzling subsides. Remove to a dish and keep warm nearby.

■ Turn the heat up to high and add the remaining 1 tablespoon oil to the wok. Add the snow peas and stir rapidly over medium heat until very hot. Season with about 1/4 teaspoon salt or to taste. Remove them to the sides and pour the well-stirred sauce into the center, stirring as it thickens. Return the scallops to the wok, add the green scallions, and stir to mix. Remove to a serving dish.

■ Serve immediately. The oyster sauce at the table is to be used to enhance the taste, while the chili sauce is used optionally.

Slippery Eggs and Shrimp

This recipe sets out the basic technique of Chinese scrambled eggs, or "slippery eggs" in Chinese. The shrimp can be omitted or replaced by diced ham or cooked crabmeat. In China, uncooked shrimp would be marinated in salt, egg white, and cornstarch, chilled for several hours, then lightly cooked before they are added to the beaten egg. But in the West, frozen cooked shrimp are readily available, so I have adapted the recipe to use cooked shrimp.

INGREDIENTS

6 large eggs
1/3–1/2 teaspoon salt
1 teaspoon sesame oil
3 scallions, cut into small rounds, green and white parts separated
About 1 cup vegetable oil
8 ounces peeled cooked frozen shrimp, thoroughly defrosted, if frozen and patted dry

METHOD

■ Beat the eggs until well mixed. Add the salt, sesame oil, and green scallions and mix well.

■ Heat the wok over a high heat until smoke rises. Add 1 tablespoon of the oil and whirl it around. Add the white scallions and stir a few times to release its aroma. Remove the wok from the heat, add the shrimp, and stir to mix. Return the wok over a low heat and stir the shrimp for another 20–30 seconds, or until they are just warm. (As they are already cooked, reheating over a high heat would make them rubbery.) Remove and mix into the beaten eggs. Wash and dry the wok.

■ Reheat the wok over a high heat until smoke rises. Pour in about 3/4 cup oil, swirl it around reaching halfway up the slope of the wok, then pour back into a container for another use. This prevents the eggs from sticking to the wok when they cook.

■ Add 4 tablespoons of the oil and swirl it around several times. Lower the heat to medium. Pour in the egg mixture and, going to the bottom of the wok with the wok scoop or a metal spatula, fold over the egg as soon as it is set, giving room for the still-runny eggs to be cooked. At the same time, drizzle 1 tablespoon oil around the side of the wok to make the eggs that much more slippery in texture. Serve immediately.

NOTE This dish goes well with rice but is equally delicious served on toast.

Shredded Pork with Cucumber

By using or not using the spicy, hot green chiles, this family dish can suit all palates. Either way, it is appetizing.

INGREDIENTS

12 ounces lean pork, pat dried, cut into strips about 2 inches long and 1/4 inch thick
4 1/2 tablespoons vegetable oil
2–3 thin slices fresh ginger, peeled
1 cucumber, about 12 ounces–16 ounces, cut as for french fries
1/2 teaspoon salt
3 fresh green chiles, seeded or unseeded, cut into small rounds (optional)
2–3 large garlic cloves, cut into strips
3–4 large scallions, cut into 2-inch sections, white and green parts separated
1 tablespoon Shaoxing wine or medium-dry sherry

MARINADE

1/2 teaspoon salt
1/4 teaspoon sugar
2 teaspoons thin soy sauce
6–8 turns white pepper mill
2 teaspoons Shaoxing wine or medium-dry sherry
1 1/2 teaspoons cornstarch
2 teaspoons vegetable oil

SAUCE

1 teaspoon cornstarch
1 1/2 teaspoons thick soy sauce
4 tablespoons water

METHOD

■ Add the salt, sugar, soy sauce, pepper, wine or sherry, and cornstarch to the pork and stir to coat well. Leave to stand for 15–20 minutes. Blend in the oils.

■ Mix together the sauce ingredients and set aside.

■ Heat the wok over a high heat until smoke rises. Add 1 1/2 tablespoons of the oil and swirl it around. Add the ginger, let sizzle, then add the cucumber. Season with the salt and stir continuously for about 1 1/2 minutes, or until very hot. Remove onto a plate and keep warm. Wipe dry the wok.

■ Reheat the wok over a high heat until smoke rises. Add the remaining 3 tablespoons oil and swirl it around several times. Add the chilies, if using, and stir a couple of times. Add the garlic, let sizzle, then add the white scallions, and stir a few times to release the aroma. Add the pork and, going to the bottom of the wok with the wok scoop or a metal spatula, flip and toss continuously for about 1 minute, or until the pork is whitish in color. Splash in the wine or sherry around the side of the wok, continuing to stir. When the sizzling dies down, add the well-stirred sauce, stirring as it thickens. Return the cucumber to the wok and add the green scallions. Stir to mix until very hot again. Remove to a serving plate and serve immediately.

Stir-Fried Pork with Leeks

Leeks cut up and separated into single rings can be very tender when stir-fried. When they are then combined with pork, they make a delicious dish together.

INGREDIENTS

1 pound lean pork, cut into rectangular pieces about 3/4 x 2 inches and 1/8 inch thick

6 tablespoons vegetable oil

1 pound leeks, trimmed, cut into 3/4-inch rounds, separated, and washed thoroughly

Salt

3 large garlic cloves, sliced diagonally into thin pieces

1 tablespoon Shaoxing wine or medium-dry sherry

MARINADE

1/3 teaspoon salt

1/4 teaspoon sugar

1 tablespoon thin soy sauce

8 turns white pepper mill

2 teaspoons Shaoxing wine or medium-dry sherry

1 1/2 teaspoons cornstarch

1 tablespoon water

1 tablespoon vegetable oil

1 teaspoon sesame oil

SAUCE

1 teaspoon cornstarch

5 tablespoons water

1–2 tablespoons oyster sauce or 2–3 teaspoons thick soy sauce

METHOD

■ Marinate the pork. Add the salt, sugar, soy sauce, pepper, wine or sherry, and cornstarch to the pork and stir to coat. Add the water and stir until it is absorbed. Leave to stand for about 20 minutes, then blend in the oils.

■ Make the sauce by mixing together the ingredients and set aside.

■ Heat the wok over a high heat until smoke rises. Add 2 tablespoons oil and swirl it around. Add the leeks, stir for about 1 minute, lowering the heat to medium so as not to burn them. Season with about 1/4–1/2 teaspoon salt, then cover, and cook in their own juice for about 2 minutes. Stir thoroughly again and continue to cook, covered, for another 2–3 minutes, until the leeks are tender. Remove onto a plate and keep warm nearby. Wipe dry the wok.

■ Reheat the wok over a high heat until smoke rises. Add the remaining 4 tablespoons oil and swirl it around. Add the garlic, let sizzle and take on color. Add the pork and, going to the bottom of the wok with the wok scoop or metal spatula, toss and turn for about 1 minute, or until the pork is partially cooked. Splash in the wine or sherry around the side of the wok, continuing to stir as it sizzles. Lower the heat, push the pork to the sloping side, and pour the well-stirred sauce into the center, stirring as it thickens. Fold in the pork, which should be cooked by now, and return the leek, stirring to mix. Remove to a serving plate and serve immediately.

Beef with Snow Peas

This recipe can be used as a guideline for stir-fried beef with other green vegetables. The snow peas can be replaced by iceberg or cos lettuce, broccoli, green beans, or even spinach. When using broccoli or green beans, however, blanch them (step 2) longer (2–4 minutes), until they are tender yet still crisp.

INGREDIENTS

8 ounces trimmed beef (fillet, rump, or skirt), cut across the grain into rectangular slices about 3/4 x 1 1/2 inches and 1/4 inch thick

1 teaspoon salt

5 tablespoons vegetable oil

8–12 ounces snow peas

2–3 large garlic cloves, cut diagonally into thin slices

3–4 thin slices fresh ginger, peeled

3–4 scallions, cut into 1-inch sections, white and green parts separated

1 tablespoon Shaoxing wine or medium-dry sherry

MARINADE

1/4 teaspoon salt

1/4 teaspoon sugar

2–3 teaspoons thick soy sauce

6–8 turns black pepper mill

1 teaspoon Shaoxing wine or medium-dry sherry

1 1/2 teaspoons cornstarch

1 tablespoon water

1 teaspoon sesame oil

SAUCE

3/4 teaspoon cornstarch

3 tablespoons water

1 1/2 tablespoons oyster sauce or 1 tablespoon thick soy sauce

METHOD

■ Marinate the beef. Add the salt, sugar, soy sauce, pepper, wine or sherry, and cornstarch to the beef and stir in the same direction to coat. Add the water, stirring until completely absorbed. Leave to stand in the refrigerator for 15–30 minutes. Blend in the oil.

■ Mix together the sauce ingredients and set aside.

■ Half-fill the wok with water and bring to a boil. Add the salt and 1 tablespoon of the oil. Plunge in the snow peas and return to a rolling boil. Pour into a colander and refresh the snow peas under cold running water. Drain.

■ Reheat the wok over a high heat until smoke rises. Add 3 tablespoons oil and swirl it around several times. Add the garlic, let sizzle, then add the ginger and the white scallions, and stir to release their aroma. Add the beef and, sliding the wok scoop or a metal spatula to the bottom of the wok, turn and toss for about 30 seconds, or until the beef is partially cooked. Splash the wine or sherry around the side of the wok, continuing to stir. When the sizzling subsides, remove the beef, still underdone, to a dish and keep warm.

■ Add the remaining 1 tablespoon oil to the wok and swirl it around. Return the snow peas to the wok and turn and toss over a moderate heat until thoroughly hot, taking care not to burn them. Push them to the sides of the wok, pour the well-stirred sauce into the center, and stir as it thickens. Return the beef to the sauce, stirring to mix. Add the green scallions, stir in the snow peas from the sides. Remove to a serving plate and serve immediately.

Beef with Pineapple

Because of the warm climate in South China, tropical fruits abound, and it is not unusual to combine fruit with meat or poultry. Pineapples and mangoes are favorites with beef, affecting an appetizingly sweet-and-sour taste in the dish.

INGREDIENTS

4 large rounds of fresh pineapple, 1/2 inch thick, cored and cut into chunks

Small pinch salt

About 2 teaspoons sugar

1 pound rump steak or skirt, trimmed and cut across the grain into rectangular slices about 3/4 x 1 1/2 inches and 1/4 inch thick

5 1/2 tablespoons vegetable oil

2 large garlic cloves, cut diagonally into thin slices

3 scallions, cut into 1-inch sections, white and green parts separated

8 thin slices peeled fresh ginger, cut into very fine silky strips

1 tablespoon Shaoxing wine or medium-dry sherry

3/4 teaspoon cornstarch dissolved in 2 tablespoons water

MARINADE

1/2 teaspoon salt

1/4 teaspoon sugar

1 tablespoon thick soy sauce

8 turns black pepper mill

2 teaspoons Shaoxing wine or medium-dry sherry

1 1/2 teaspoons cornstarch

1–2 tablespoons water

1 teaspoon sesame oil

METHOD

■ Taste the pineapple for acidity, then add the salt and sugar accordingly. Mix well and leave to stand for 30 minutes or longer.

■ Marinate the beef. Add the salt, sugar, soy sauce, pepper, wine or sherry and cornstarch to the beef and stir in the same direction to coat. Add the water, 1 tablespoonful at a time, stirring until completely absorbed before adding another spoonful. Leave to stand in the refrigerator for 15–20 minutes. Blend in the oil.

■ Heat the wok over a high heat until smoke rises. Add 4 tablespoons of the oil and swirl it around several times. Add the garlic, let sizzle, then add the white scallions and half of the ginger; stir to release their aroma. Add the beef and, sliding the wok scoop or a metal spatula to the bottom of the wok, turn and toss for about 30 seconds, or until the beef is partially cooked. Splash the wine or sherry around the side of the wok. When the sizzling subsides, remove the beef, still underdone, to a dish and keep warm nearby.

■ Add the remaining 1 1/2 tablespoons oil to the wok and swirl it around over a high heat. Add the remaining ginger, stir a few times, then add the pineapple. Push the pineapple to the edges and pour the well-stirred dissolved cornstarch into the center of the wok, continuing to stir as it thickens. Return the beef to the wok, add the green scallions, and stir to mix until thoroughly hot again. Remove onto a serving dish and serve immediately.

Chicken in Black Bean Sauce

The Chinese love to suck chicken bones, and they often chop the bird into fairly small pieces, either before or after cooking it. When stir-fried with black beans and lots of garlic, the chicken pieces are scrumptious.

INGREDIENTS

1 chicken, 2 1/4–2 1/2 pounds, cleaned, chopped through skin and bones into 1-inch pieces
4 tablespoons vegetable oil
1 medium-sized green pepper, seeded and roughly chopped
Salt to taste
15–20 garlic cloves
4 large scallions, cut into 2-inch sections, white and green parts separated
3–3 1/2 tablespoons preserved black beans, 2 tablespoons mashed and 1 tablespoon left whole (see page 22)
1 tablespoon Shaoxing wine or medium-dry sherry
1 1/2 teaspoons cornstarch dissolved in 4 tablespoons water

MARINADE

1/2 teaspoon salt
1/2 teaspoon sugar
1 tablespoon thin soy sauce
8 turns black pepper mill
2 teaspoons Shaoxing wine or medium-dry sherry

METHOD

■ Marinate the chicken. Add the salt, sugar, soy sauce, pepper, and wine or sherry to the chicken and mix thoroughly. Leave to stand for about 30 minutes. Separate the white breast pieces from the rest.

■ Heat the wok over a high heat until smoke rises. Add 1/2 tablespoon of the oil and swirl it around. Add the green pepper, season with a pinch of salt, and stir for about 1 minute over medium heat. Remove and keep nearby.

■ Reheat the wok over a high heat until smoke rises. Add the remaining 3 1/2 tablespoons oil and swirl it around several times. Add the garlic, fry for about 30 seconds, or until it takes on color. Add the white scallions, stir a few times, then add the black beans and stir together to release their aroma. Add the chicken, except for the breast pieces, and, going to the bottom of the wok with a wok scoop or a metal spatula, turn and toss vigorously for about 2 minutes. Add the breast pieces and continue to turn and toss for another minute. Splash the wine or sherry around the sides of the wok, stirring all the time. When the sizzling subsides, lower the heat to medium, put on the wok lid, and continue to cook for about 4 minutes. Remove the lid and stir, turning over the pieces, which should have oozed out juices. Taste the dark meat for readiness, then continue to cook, covered, for another 3–5 minutes, or until just cooked.

■ Remove the lid, return the green pepper to the wok, and stir together with the chicken until hot. Pour in the well-stirred dissolved cornstarch, stirring as it thickens. Add the green scallions, mix, and serve immediately.

Chicken with Celery and Cashew Nuts

This is a combination that greatly pleases the Western palate. The Chinese also like it, but don't necessarily always include the cashew nuts. The crunchiness of the celery and the nuts provides contrast to the tenderness of the chicken. Texture is the essence of Chinese cooking.

INGREDIENTS

12 ounces skinned and boned chicken breast, cut into slices about 1/3 inch thick

5 tablespoons vegetable oil

4 ribs celery, cut diagonally into slices about 1/8 inch thick

Salt

2–3 large garlic cloves, sliced diagonally

3 scallions, cut into 1-inch sections, white and green parts separated

1 tablespoon Shaoxing wine or medium-dry sherry

1/2 cup roasted cashew nuts

MARINADE

1/3 teaspoon salt

1/4 teaspoon sugar

2 teaspoons thin soy sauce

8 turns white pepper mill

2 teaspoons Shaoxing wine or medium-dry sherry

1 teaspoon cornstarch

1 tablespoon egg white

2 teaspoons vegetable oil

1 teaspoon sesame oil

SAUCE

1 1/2 teaspoons cornstarch

5 tablespoons water

1 tablespoon oyster sauce or 2 teaspoons thick soy sauce

METHOD

■ Marinate the chicken. Add the salt, sugar, soy sauce, pepper, and wine or sherry to the chicken and mix to coat. Sprinkle with the cornstarch, add the egg white, and stir to coat well. Leave to stand for 15–20 minutes. Blend in the oils.

■ Mix together the sauce ingredients and set aside.

■ Heat the wok over a high heat until smoke rises. Add 1 tablespoon of the oil and swirl it around. Add the celery and stir rapidly for 1 minute, seasoning with a pinch of salt. The celery should be crunchy, even though cooked. Remove and keep warm nearby. Wipe dry the wok.

■ Reheat the wok over a high heat until smoke rises. Add the remaining 4 tablespoons of oil and swirl it around. Add the garlic, let sizzle, then add the white scallions, and stir a few times to release their aroma. Add the chicken and, going to the bottom of the wok with the scoop or metal spatula, flip and turn for 30–60 seconds, or until the chicken is becoming opaque. Splash in the wine or sherry around the side of the wok, continuing to stir as it sizzles. Add the well-stirred sauce and continue to stir until it thickens. Return the celery to the wok, add the nuts and the green scallions, and stir to mix. Remove to a serving plate and serve immediately.

Lambs' Kidneys in Marsala Sauce

Lambs' kidney, subtle in taste and texture, can easily become rubbery if it is overcooked. By stir-frying it, however, you can cook it to a turn, or even have it slightly underdone. In this recipe, the interaction between the salt, ginger juice, sesame oil, and Marsala wine produces a scrumptious result. This recipe serves 2 as a main course.

INGREDIENTS

6 lambs' kidneys
4 tablespoons vegetable oil
3 large garlic cloves, cut diagonally into thin slices
2–2 1/2 tablespoons Marsala wine
1 teaspoon cornstarch dissolved in 3 tablespoons water
1 ounce flaked almond
MARINADE
1 teaspoon salt
Black pepper to taste
2 teaspoons fresh ginger juice (see page 25)
1 tablespoon sesame oil

METHOD

■ Carefully remove the white fatty lumps and membranes of the kidneys. Cut each horizontally into about 6 pieces, removing any remaining white membranes. Put into a bowl.

■ Marinate the kidneys. Add the salt, pepper, and ginger juice to the kidneys and mix well. Leave to stand for about 30 minutes. Blend in the oil.

■ Heat the wok over a high heat until smoke rises. Add the oil and swirl it around several times. Add the garlic, let sizzle and take on color, then add the kidneys. Sliding the wok scoop or a metal spatula to the bottom of the wok, flip and turn continuously for 1 1/2 minutes, until the pieces begin to turn opaque. Splash in the Marsala wine around the side of the wok and, as it sizzles, continue to stir for another 1 1/2 minutes. Lower the heat to medium, pour in the well-stirred dissolved cornstarch, and stir as it thickens. Continue to cook for another 30–60 seconds, and then remove to a serving dish. The kidney is slightly underdone and juicy. Sprinkle with the almonds and serve.

VARIATION: VEAL KIDNEY IN MARSALA SAUCE

Use a veal kidney (about 1–1 1/4 pounds), cut horizontally into thin slices about 1/4 inch thick, then proceed as above.

Stir-Fried Milk

This strange-sounding dish originated sometime during the early part of the 20th century in Daliang, a county near Canton renowned for the ingenuity of its chefs, who exerted great influence on Cantonese cooking.

INGREDIENTS

Peanut or vegetable oil
6 ounces fresh white mushrooms, chopped
Salt
1 1/2 ounces rice sticks, broken into 2 1/2-inch lengths
3 tablespoons cornstarch
2 1/2 cups whole milk
6 large egg whites
4 ounces cooked crabmeat or peeled shrimp
White pepper to taste
1–2 ounces ham, minced

METHOD

■ Heat the wok over a high heat until smoke rises. Add 1 tablespoon of the oil and swirl it around. Add the mushrooms, season with 1/4 teaspoon salt, and stir rapidly for 1 1/2–2 minutes, until cooked. Drain in a sieve. Wash and dry the wok.

■ Half-fill the wok with oil and heat to 350° F, or until 1 rice stick rises to the surface instantly. Add the rice sticks, which will sink to the bottom, then rise to the surface, expanding into a snow-white woven mass. Gently press them down once with a large hand strainer or perforated disc to make sure that they are thoroughly deep-fried. Remove at once to drain on paper towels, then transfer to line a large serving plate. Pour the oil into a container for another use. Wash and dry the wok.

■ Dissolve the cornstarch in 3–4 tablespoons of the milk.

■ Gently stir the egg whites. Stir in the remaining milk, crabmeat, and mushrooms. Season with 1/2–3/4 teaspoon salt and white pepper to taste. Add the well-stirred dissolved cornstarch.

■ Reheat the wok over a high heat until smoke rises. Add 7 tablespoons clean and unused oil and swirl it to halfway up the wok. Give the milk mixture one more stir and pour into the wok. Lower the heat and, using the back of the wok scoop, move the liquid mixture away from the sides, towards the center. As it slowly solidifies, let the still-runny mixture go to the sides and bottom to be cooked, taking care that it does not stick. As soon as it has all set, remove from the heat, and spoon onto the rice sticks. Sprinkle with ham and serve.

NOTE Take care not to overcook the milk or water will start oozing out.

Family Bean Curd

So called when the bean curd, cooked with a small amount of meat, either pork or beef, is seasoned harmoniously with soy sauce but without any spicy hot condiments, such as chili sauce, so that everybody in the family, old and young, with or without a highly developed palate, can eat it.

INGREDIENTS

6 ounces ground beef
4 cakes firm bean curd, each about 2 1/2 inches square and 1 1/14 inches thick
3 tablespoons vegetable oil
2 garlic cloves, finely chopped
3 scallions, cut into small rounds, white and green parts separated
1 tablespoon Shaoxing wine or medium-dry sherry
2/3 cup chicken or beef stock
1 1/2 teaspoons cornstarch dissolved in 1 tablespoon water
1–2 teaspoons sesame oil

MARINADE

3/4 teaspoon salt
1/4 teaspoon sugar
1 tablespoon thick soy sauce
6 turns black pepper mill
1 teaspoon Shaoxing wine or medium-dry sherry
1 1/2 teaspoons cornstarch
1 tablespoon water

METHOD

■ Marinate the beef. Add the salt, sugar, soy sauce, pepper, wine or sherry, and cornstarch to the beef and stir in the same direction until well coated. Add the water and stir again until absorbed. Leave to stand for 15–20 minutes.

■ Steep the bean curds in hot water for 15 minutes. Drain, handling with care. Put on paper towels to absorb all the excess water. Cut each bean curd cake into 32 cubes; quarter lengthwise and horizontally, then halve each piece.

■ Heat the wok over a high heat until smoke rises. Add the oil and swirl it around. Add the garlic, then the white scallions, and stir several times. Add the beef and, going to the bottom of the wok with the wok scoop or metal spatula, flip and toss for about 1 minute. Splash in the wine or sherry around the side of the wok, stirring continuously. When the sizzling subsides, pour in the stock, lower the heat, and let the beef simmer in the stock for 5–10 minutes. Stir in the dissolved cornstarch.

■ Add the bean curd to the meat sauce. Gently turn and fold the mixture over a medium heat until the bean curd is piping hot. Sprinkle on the green scallions. Spoon onto a serving dish. Sprinkle on the sesame oil and serve hot.

Steamed Rice

Rice is the staple food for the Chinese and can be eaten with every dish in the book. Long-grain white rice—husked and polished—is what the Chinese like to eat every single day. It is as traditional to boil rice as it is to steam it but, whereas boiled rice has a tendency to stick together, steamed rice is firmer in texture and the grains are more separate. To steam rice, use the same volume of water as rice, for example 1 cup of rice and 1 cup of water. One cup of uncooked rice yields about 3 loose cups of cooked rice.

This recipe is the basis for more fancy rice dishes, such as Shrimp Fried Rice and Mixed Fried Rice (see pages 85 and 86).

INGREDIENTS

2 cups long-grain white rice
2 cups water
1 tablespoon vegetable oil

METHOD

■ Wash the rice in several changes of water, rubbing with the fingers, until the water is no longer milky. Drain off excess water. (This can also be done in a wire under running water.)

■ Put the rice in either a cake pan or a glass pie dish. Add the water and oil. Put the pan or dish on the steaming stand in the wok.

■ Steam, covered, over a high heat for about 25 minutes in a cake pan or 35 minutes in a glass dish, at the end of which time the rice should be firm, but cooked through. Fluff up the rice and serve. It yields about 6 loose cups of rice.

Shrimp-Fried Rice

In China one would always use raw shrimp, but for convenience I have used cooked shrimp in this recipe. Just make sure that you simply heat them through and don't cook them too rapidly.

INGREDIENTS

6 cups cooked rice, loosely packed (see previous page)
8 ounces frozen green peas (1 1/2 cups)
8 ounces cooked shrimps
5 tablespoons vegetable oil
2 garlic cloves, finely chopped
1 teaspoon salt
6 scallions, chopped, white and green parts separated
1 very large or 2 small eggs, lightly beaten
Thin or thick soy sauce

METHOD

▪ Leave the cooked rice, covered, for 4–5 hours or overnight. Loosen the grains, breaking up lumps just before use.

▪ Blanch the peas in a pot of salted water for 2–3 minutes. Drain well. If frozen cooked shrimp are used, defrost and then pat dry.

▪ Heat the wok over a high heat until smoke rises. Add 1 1/2 tablespoons of the oil and swirl it around. Add the garlic, which will sizzle, taking on color. Add the shrimp, season with 1/2 teaspoon of salt and stir rapidly for 30–60 seconds, until hot, in order to incorporate the oil and fragrance. Do not overcook them lest they become tough and chewy. Remove to a dish and keep warm nearby. Wipe dry the wok.

▪ Reheat the wok over a high heat until smoke rises. Add the remaining 3 1/2 tablespoons oil and swirl it around. Add the white scallions and stir a few times. Pour in the egg and let it set at the bottom for a few seconds while the surface is still runny. Add the well-loosened rice and, going to the bottom of the wok with the wok scoop or metal spatula, flip and turn rapidly for 2–3 minutes, or until the rice is thoroughly hot. Add the remaining 1/2 teaspoon salt and the peas, continuing to stir until piping hot again. Return the shrimp to the wok, add the green scallions, and stir to mix. Transfer to a serving bowl or dish and serve immediately. Thin or thick soy sauce can be added at the table to suit individual taste.

Mixed Fried Rice

A delicious fried rice dish fit for guests and family as the main course for 4–5 people, to be washed down with beer, cider, or white wine. You can vary the ingredients and use up leftovers as long as you keep the basics—rice, scallions, and egg.

INGREDIENTS

2/3 cup frozen green peas

6 tablespoons vegetable oil

4 ounces canned bamboo shoots, diced

1 small cucumber, peeled, seeded, and diced

4–6 scallions, chopped, white and green parts separated

2 eggs, lightly beaten with 1/4 teaspoon salt

6 cups cooked rice, loosely packed (see page 84), grains loosened and separated

1/2 teaspoon salt

1 1/2 pounds bacon, diced, cooked, and drained

2 cups diced roast chicken

1 tablespoon thin soy sauce, or to taste

METHOD

■ Blanch the peas in a pot of boiling salted water for 2–3 minutes. Drain well.

■ Heat the wok over a high heat until smoke rises. Add 2 tablespoons of the oil and swirl it around. Add the bamboo shoots and cucumber. Stir and turn rapidly for 1–2 minutes, until piping hot. Remove to a dish and mix in the peas. Wash and dry the wok.

■ Reheat the wok over a high heat until smoke rises. Add the remaining 4 tablespoons oil and swirl it around several times. Add the white scallions and stir to release their aroma. Pour in the eggs and leave for a few seconds to set partially. Add the rice. (The eggs will be half runny and will moisten the rice.) Sliding the wok scoop or a metal spatula to the bottom of the wok, flip and turn rapidly until the rice is hot. Season with the salt and add the bacon and chicken, continuing to stir until the mixture is hot again. Add the soy sauce and green scallions. Stir to mix, test for taste, then spoon into a large serving bowl. Serve immediately.

Green Beans with Garlic

If it seems a lot of garlic for a pound of beans, do not be alarmed, for the Chinese way of frying the garlic in hot oil releases its aroma, which is then transmitted to the beans. The result is a special "wok fragrance" in the beans without the unpleasant odor associated with garlic. The same principle can be applied to preparing shell beans, although they should be blanched for a little longer.

INGREDIENTS

Salt

5 tablespoons vegetable oil

1 pound green beans, trimmed

6 large garlic cloves, finely chopped

2 teaspoons thin soy sauce

METHOD

■ Half-fill the wok with boiling water and keep it boiling. Add 1 teaspoon salt and 1 1/2 tablespoons of oil, which will preserve the vivid color of the beans when cooked. Add the beans and blanch for 2–4 minutes, depending on size; they should still have a bite to them. Pour into a colander and immediately rinse thoroughly under cold running water in order to retain their crisp texture. Drain.

■ Dry the wok. Reheat over a high heat until smoke rises. Add the remaining oil and swirl it around. Add the garlic, stir as it sizzles and takes on color. Add the beans and, going to the bottom of the wok with the wok scoop, flip and turn rapidly for 1–2 minutes, or until the beans are thoroughly hot. Adjust the heat, if necessary, so that the beans do not burn. Add the soy sauce, stir to mix, then remove to a serving plate, and serve hot.

Stir-Fried Bean Sprouts

INGREDIENTS

1 pound bean sprouts
3–4 tablespoons vegetable oil
3 slices fresh ginger, peeled
2–3 scallions, cut into 1-inch sections, white and green parts separated
1/2 teaspoon salt
2 teaspoons thin soy sauce

METHOD

- Rinse the bean sprouts and drain well. Trim the root ends.

- Heat the wok over a high heat until smoke rises. Add the oil and swirl it around. Add the ginger, then the white scallions, and let sizzle for a few seconds to release their aroma. Add the bean sprouts and, sliding the wok scoop to the bottom of the wok, flip and turn for about 3 minutes. Then add the salt and soy sauce. Add the green scallions, stir, and remove to a serving plate. Serve immediately.

Stir-Fried Napa Cabbage

Napa cabbage may be called Chinese cabbage, Chinese celery cabbage, or Chinese leaves, but you should be able to find it at your local supermarket.

INGREDIENTS

4 tablespoons vegetable oil
1 1/2 pounds napa cabbage, leaves and stems separated and sliced 1/2-inch thick
3 slices fresh ginger, peeled
2–3 scallions, cut into 1-inch sections, white and green parts separated
1/2 teaspoon salt
1 tablespoon thin soy sauce

METHOD

■ Heat the wok over a high heat until smoke rises. Add the oil and swirl it around. Add the ginger, then the white scallions, and let sizzle for a few seconds to release their aroma. Add the cabbage stems and, sliding the wok scoop to the bottom of the wok, flip and turn for about 2 minutes. Then add the leaves and stir-fry for another 2 minutes. Reduce the heat, cover the wok with the lid, and cook for 4 minutes. Add the salt and soy sauce. Add the green scallions, stir, and remove to a serving plate. Serve immediately.

Stir-Fried Green Cabbage

INGREDIENTS

3 tablespoons vegetable oil
3 slices fresh ginger, peeled
2–3 scallions, cut into 1-inch sections, white and green parts separated
1 1/2 pounds green cabbage, roughly chopped
1/2 teaspoon salt
2 teaspoons thin soy sauce

METHOD

■ Heat the wok over a high heat until smoke rises. Add the oil and swirl it around. Add the ginger, then the white scallions, and let sizzle for a few seconds to release their aroma. Add the cabbage and, sliding the wok scoop to the bottom of the wok, flip and turn for 3–5 minutes. Then reduce the heat, cover the wok with the lid, and cook for 3–5 more minutes, until tender but still slightly crunchy. Add the salt and soy sauce. Add the green scallions, stir, and remove to a serving plate. Serve immediately.

Stir-Fried Lettuce

Although lettuce is most commonly eaten raw in salads and sandwiches in the West, it is delicious quickly cooked Chinese-style in a wok.

INGREDIENTS

3 tablespoons vegetable oil
3 slices fresh ginger, peeled
2–3 scallions, cut into 1-inch sections, white and green parts separated
1 large head cos or iceberg lettuce, broken into large pieces
1/2 teaspoon salt
2 teaspoons oyster sauce

METHOD

■ Heat the wok over a high heat until smoke rises. Add the oil and swirl it around. Add the ginger, then the white scallions, and let sizzle for a few seconds to release their aroma. Add the lettuce and, sliding the wok scoop to the bottom of the wok, flip and turn for 2–3 minutes. Then add the salt and oyster sauce. Add the green scallions, stir, and remove to a serving plate. Serve immediately.

Stir-Fried Celery

INGREDIENTS

2 1/2–3 tablespoons vegetable oil
3 slices fresh ginger, peeled
2–3 scallions, cut into 1-inch sections, white and green parts separated
1 bunch celery, sliced on the diagonal 1/4 inch thick
1/2–3/4 teaspoon salt

METHOD

• Heat the wok over a high heat until smoke rises. Add the oil and swirl it around. Add the ginger, then the white scallions, and let sizzle for a few seconds to release their aroma. Add the celery and, sliding the wok scoop to the bottom of the wok, flip and turn for 1–1 1/2 minutes. Then add the salt and green scallions, stir, and remove to a serving plate. Serve immediately.

Stir-Fried Cucumber

Look for the long English or European cucumbers that come wrapped in plastic; these aren't waxed and can be enjoyed with the peels still on for better texture.

INGREDIENTS

3 tablespoons vegetable oil
3 slices fresh ginger, peeled
2–3 scallions, cut into 1-inch sections, white and green parts separated
1 long English or European cucumber (not waxed), cut in sticks as for french fries
1/2 teaspoon salt

METHOD

■ Heat the wok over a high heat until smoke rises. Add the oil and swirl it around. Add the ginger, then the white scallions, and let sizzle for a few seconds to release their aroma. Add the cucumber and, sliding the wok scoop to the bottom of the wok, flip and turn for 2–3 minutes. Then add the salt and green scallions, stir, and remove to a serving plate. Serve immediately.

Stir-Fried Spinach

INGREDIENTS

1 pound spinach

5 tablespoons vegetable oil

4–5 garlic cloves, finely chopped

1/2–3/4 teaspoon salt

METHOD

■ Bring a large pan of water to a boil. Add 1 tablespoon oil. Add the spinach and blanch for 20 seconds. Pour into a colander and drain.

■ Heat the wok over a high heat until smoke rises. Add the oil and swirl it around. Add the garlic and let sizzle for a few seconds to release their aroma. Add the spinach and, sliding the wok scoop to the bottom of the wok, flip and turn for 6–7 minutes. Then add the salt, stir, and remove to a serving plate. Serve immediately.

Stir-Fried Fresh Mushrooms

INGREDIENTS

| 2 tablespoons vegetable oil |
| 2–3 scallions, cut into 1-inch sections, white and green parts separated |
| 8 ounces mushrooms, sliced |
| 1/4–1/3 teaspoon salt |

METHOD

■ Heat the wok over a high heat until smoke rises. Add the oil and swirl it around. Add the white scallions, and let sizzle for a few seconds to release their aroma. Add the mushrooms and, sliding the wok scoop to the bottom of the wok, flip and turn for 2–4 minutes. Then add the salt and green scallions, stir, and remove to a serving plate. Serve immediately.

95

Stir-Fried Zucchini

Zucchini is not a Chinese vegetable, but if sliced thinly, it can be adapted to wok stir-frying most successfully. In fact, cooked this way, not only will the vivid color of the vegetable be retained, but a crisp texture will be introduced. To achieve this effect, however, it is important to draw out the water beforehand, thereby getting rid of its slightly bitter taste, as well as preventing it from going soggy in a pool of liquid when cooked.

INGREDIENTS

1 pound medium-sized zucchini
About 1 1/4 teaspoons salt
3 tablespoons vegetable oil
4 thin slices fresh ginger, peeled
2–3 scallions, cut into 1-inch sections, white and green parts separated
1–2 teaspoons thin soy sauce

METHOD

■ Wash the zucchini, cut and discard the tops and ends. Slice horizontally into thin slivers no more than 1/8 inch thick. Put into a large bowl. Sprinkle with the salt and mix thoroughly. Leave to stand for about 20 minutes, or until water has been drawn out. Drain but leave damp.

■ Heat the wok over a high heat until smoke rises. Add the oil and swirl it around. Add the ginger, then the white scallions, and let sizzle for a few seconds to release their aroma. Add the zucchini and, sliding the wok scoop to the bottom of the wok, flip and turn for about 1 minute. Lower the heat to medium and continue to turn and toss for about 3 minutes, or until the zucchini is tender, yet still has a bite to it. Test for taste, then add the soy sauce. Add the green scallions, stir, and remove to a serving plate. Serve immediately.

Steamed Grey Mullet (Steaming: page 26).

Steamed Siu Mai (Steaming: page 44).

Shrimp in Black Bean Sauce (Stir-frying: page 60).

Shredded Pork with Cucumber and Stir-fried Mixed Vegetables
(Stir-frying: page 66).

Beef with Snow Peas (Stir-frying: page 70).

Bean Curd with Pork (Sautéing: page 124) with Steamed Rice (page 84)
and Sauté Pouch Egg (page 130).

Shrimp Toasts (Deep-frying: page 134).

Madame So's Wok-roast Chicken (Braising: page 151).

Chinese Broccoli with Ginger Juice

Compared to ordinary broccoli, Chinese broccoli is more subtle in taste, reminiscent of asparagus. This subtle taste is further enhanced by the infusion of the mixture of ginger juice and Shaoxing wine. If Chinese broccoli is not available, ordinary broccoli can be used instead, and its taste will also benefit from the wine and ginger juice. Chinese broccoli is also known as *gai lan* (Cantonese) and Chinese kale.

INGREDIENTS

1 pound Chinese broccoli, washed and trimmed
Salt
4 tablespoons vegetable oil
1–1 1/2 inches fresh ginger, peeled and finely chopped
1 tablespoon Shaoxing wine or medium-dry sherry
2 tablespoons oyster sauce

METHOD

■ Break up the leafy parts of the broccoli and cut the stalks diagonally at 1/2-inch intervals. Leave the florets whole.

■ Bring a large pan of water to a boil, and add 1 teaspoon salt and 1 tablespoon oil. Add the broccoli, return to a boil, then continue to boil for 2 minutes. The broccoli will still be very crunchy. Pour into a colander and drain.

■ Put the ginger, in several batches, into a garlic press, add 2 drops of water each time and squeeze the juice into a small bowl, scraping the minced ginger found on the surface of the press as well. Discard the pulp inside. Add the wine or sherry to the juice.

■ Heat the wok over a high heat until smoke rises. Add the remaining oil and swirl it around. Tip in the drained broccoli and stir to mix with the oil in the wok. Pour in the ginger juice with wine or sherry and sprinkle on a pinch of salt. Sliding the wok scoop or metal spatula to the bottom of the wok, flip and turn to allow the ginger juice and wine to be absorbed. Lower the heat to medium, add a little water (about 1 tablespoon), and cook, covered, for another minute. The broccoli should be crisp but not hard. Remove to a serving plate and drizzle over the oyster sauce. Serve hot.

Button Mushroom Vinaigrette

This mushroom vinaigrette, with its faint but refreshing ginger taste, is a winner as a first course or a side dish—especially for those who do not care for garlic in a vinaigrette sauce. It is usually served cold, but this dish is also very good hot. The sauce is rich and rather tart. When cold, serve it with cold roast pork as a side dish.

INGREDIENTS

5 tablespoons vegetable oil
8–10 scallions, chopped, white and green parts separated
1 1/4 pound small button mushrooms, washed and trimmed
1 inch fresh ginger, peeled and finely chopped
1 teaspoon salt
1 teaspoon sugar
3 tablespoons white wine vinegar

METHOD

■ Heat the wok over a high heat until smoke rises. Add the oil and swirl it around. Add the white scallions and let them sizzle, releasing their aroma. Add the mushrooms and, sliding the wok scoop or a metal spatula to the bottom of the wok, turn and toss the mushrooms constantly for about 1 minute. Lower the heat to medium and continue to cook the mushrooms, which will gradually start oozing out water.

■ Put the ginger into a garlic press in about 3 batches, adding 2–3 drops of water each time, and squeeze the juice over the mushrooms. Add the minced ginger that was squeezed through the press as well, discarding the pulp inside. Add the salt, sugar, and 2 tablespoons of the vinegar. Continue to cook the mushrooms for about 10 minutes over a fairly high heat, stirring from time to time. At the end of the cooking, the sauce should be rich and tart. Add the remaining vinegar and the green scallions, and stir to mix.

■ Remove from the wok, allow to cool, then chill in the refrigerator for several hours or overnight. Serve cold.

Stir-Fried Creamed Cauliflower

The Western influence in this 20th-century Chinese recipe is evident in the use of evaporated milk or cream. Use of the traditional chicken fat , when combined with the milk or cream, lends an added flavor to the vegetable.

INGREDIENTS

1 head cauliflower, 1 1/2–2 pounds
7 cups water
1 teaspoon salt
1 tablespoon vegetable oil
3–4 tablespoons rendered chicken fat or 3–4 tablespoons vegetable oil
2–3 thin slices fresh ginger, peeled
2–3 scallions, cut into 2-inch sections, white and green parts separated

SAUCE

1 1/2 teaspoons cornstarch
3/4 cup evaporated milk or light cream
3/4–1 teaspoon salt

METHOD

■ Cut off and discard the outer hard stalks of the cauliflower. Cut the florets into uniform bite-sized pieces.

■ Mix together the sauce ingredients and set aside.

■ Fill the wok with water and bring to a boil. Add the salt and the oil. Plunge in the cauliflower and return to a boil. Continue to boil for 3–4 minutes, or until the cauliflower is tender yet retains a bite to it. Pour into a colander and refresh under cold running water. Drain.

■ Heat the wok again over a high heat until smoke rises. Add the chicken fat or oil and swirl it around several times. Add the ginger, stir, then add the white scallions, and stir a few times to release its aroma. Return the cauliflower to the wok. Sliding the wok scoop or metal spatula to the bottom of the wok, turn and toss rapidly for about 1 minute, or until piping hot, lowering the heat so as not to burn the cauliflower. Pour in the well-stirred sauce, continuing to stir until it thickens. Add the green scallions. Remove to a serving dish and serve immediately.

Asparagus in Stock

A delicate vegetable like asparagus needs equally delicate culinary treatment. Steeping it in stock does just that, enhancing its inherent sweetness while preserving its pure taste.

INGREDIENTS

1 pound medium-sized asparagus, cleaned
1 1/4 cups concentrated but clear chicken or ham stock
1/2 teaspoon salt
3 tablespoons vegetable oil
2 teaspoons cornstarch dissolved in 1 tablespoon stock
4 thin slices fresh ginger, peeled
2–3 scallions, cut into 1-inch sections, white and green parts separated

METHOD

■ Chop off and discard the hard end of each asparagus stem. Halve the remainder. Split vertically halfway down the thicker bottom half, ensuring more even cooking.

■ Pour the stock into the wok and bring it to a boil. Add the salt and 1 tablespoon of the oil. Add the asparagus, return to a boil, then continue to cook over a gentle heat for about 3 minutes. Carefully transfer the asparagus and stock to a bowl and leave the asparagus to steep in the stock for about 1–2 hours. The asparagus will be tender, yet still have a bite to them. Then lift them out of the stock onto a dish.

■ Stir the dissolved cornstarch into half of the stock, saving the remainder for another use.

■ Reheat the cleaned wok over a high heat until smoke rises. Add the remaining 2 tablespoons oil and swirl it around. Add the ginger, stir, then add the white scallions. Lowering the heat to medium, return the asparagus to the wok and stir until thoroughly hot. Pour in the well-stirred stock, continuing to stir as it thickens. Mix in the green scallions, then transfer to a serving dish. Serve immediately.

Stir-Fried Mixed Vegetables

The choice of vegetables to stir-fry together is really up to you. Be imaginative: Give the dish a visual appeal; also make some contrast of texture among the vegetables. Take this recipe as a guideline, and add or subtract a vegetable as you like. When the vegetables are leafy and tender, there is no need to blanch them either.

INGREDIENTS

2 teaspoons salt
5 tablespoons vegetable oil
6 ounces green beans, trimmed and halved crossways if long (about 1 1/4 cups)
12 ounces green cabbage, cored and cut into fairly large pieces (about 5 cups)
6 ounces carrots, peeled and cut into both large and thin slices (2 1/2 medium-sized)
4 ounces canned bamboo shoots, cut into both large and thin slices
3–4 thin slices fresh ginger, peeled
3–4 scallions, cut into 2-inch sections, white and green parts separated
2–3 teaspoons thin soy sauce

METHOD

■ Pour a kettle of boiling water into the wok and bring to a boil. Add 1 1/2 teaspoons of the salt and 1 1/2 tablespoons of the oil. Add the green beans, return to a boil, then continue to blanch for about 2 minutes. Add the cabbage, carrots, and bamboo shoots, return to a boil, then continue to cook for 2 more minutes. Pour into a colander and refresh under cold running water in order to retain the crispness and vivid color of the vegetables. Drain. (This step can be done a couple of hours in advance.)

■ Dry the wok. Reheat over a high heat until smoke rises. Add the remaining 3 1/2 tablespoons of oil and swirl it around. Add the ginger, stir, then add the white scallions, and stir a few times. Return all the vegetables to the wok and, going to the bottom of the wok with the wok scoop or metal spatula, turn and toss for about 2 minutes, or until the vegetables are tender yet still crunchy. Adjust the heat if the cabbage begins to burn. Season with the remaining 1/2 teaspoon salt and the soy sauce. Add the green scallions. Remove onto a serving dish and serve hot.

SAUTÉING
AND PAN-FRYING

▲▲▲▲▲▲▲▲▲▲▲▲▲▲▲▲▲▲

The Chinese were sautéing and pan-frying by Han times (206 BC–AD 220), even though it may not have been exactly the same as modern sautéing or shallow pan-frying.

Related to deep-frying and stir-frying, pan-frying is nevertheless distinctively different from them. In deep-frying, so much oil is used that the pieces of food being deep-fried can actually swim in it, but in sautéing and pan-frying a comparatively small amount of oil is needed to cook the ingredients. True to its name, the motion of stirring is essential to the stir-frying and the ingredients are cut up into fairly small morsels; in sautéing, the ingredients may be kept in large pieces and fried *in situ*, turning halfway through the cooking time. If speed is called for in stir-frying, then patience is the secret of success in pan-frying. The food is fried slowly over a modest heat until its surface gradually turns the golden brown color it should be.

While the French sauté pans, deep with a flat bottom, are excellent, the Chinese wok, with its quick and even distribution of heat, comes up to the mark as well. Do not hesitate to tilt the wok to this side or that in order to concentrate on frying a particular section of a large ingredient. The Chinese would pan-fry a whole fish, with head and tail, in the wok. Naturally, the flame is concentrated in the center so the only way to get the fish evenly brown is to use the tilting method.

Start pan-frying with about half the oil and dribble in more oil around the ingredients as you go along or when you turn the food over. To add to the fragrance, you can splash in some rice wine or medium-dry sherry towards the end of the cooking time, just as you would for stir-frying.

Sautéed Halibut

The flavor of halibut is so delicate that it deserves an equally subtle sauce like this one, which has a very slight sweet-and-sour taste to it. Halibut is very expensive so on lean days use cod steaks.

INGREDIENTS

1 or 2 halibut steaks, about 1 pound
1 1/2–2 teaspoons fresh ginger juice (see page 25)
About 2 tablespoons cornstarch
1/2 teaspoon salt
3–4 tablespoons vegetable oil
2 garlic cloves, finely chopped
1 tablespoon Shaoxing wine or medium-dry sherry
About 1/2 inch fresh ginger, peeled and finely chopped
2 scallions, cut into small rounds

SAUCE

1 1/2 teaspoons cornstarch
6 tablespoons water
1 tablespoon thin soy sauce
2 teaspoons rice or white wine vinegar
1/4–1/2 teaspoon sugar

METHOD

■ Pat the halibut steaks dry. Rub all over with the ginger juice, piercing the flesh with a fork for better absorption. Leave to stand for 10–15 minutes.

■ Mix together the sauce ingredients and set aside.

■ Just before heating the wok, press the steaks on both sides with the cornstarch, smoothing with fingers to coat evenly. Shake off excess cornstarch.

■ Heat the wok over a high heat until smoke rises. Sprinkle with the salt, add 2 tablespoons of the oil, and swirl it around. Lower the steaks into the oil and pan-fry each side for 1–2 minutes, until golden. Add the garlic and ginger to the oil, let sizzle for a few seconds, then splash in the wine or sherry around the side of the wok. When the sizzling subsides, trickle 1–2 tablespoons of oil around the fish, loosening the edges with the wok scoop or a metal spatula. Lower the heat, put on the wok cover, and continue to cook each side for 4–5 minutes. The steaks are cooked when the flesh comes away, albeit slightly, from the main bone in the center. Remove to a serving dish, leaving a little oil behind in the wok.

■ Add the well-stirred sauce and the scallions to the wok and stir until it thickens. Spoon the sauce over the fish and serve immediately.

Fish Cakes with Broccoli

An excellent summer dish when the hot weather dampens your appetite for meat. If dried shrimp are not available, 1–2 ounces of minced ham can be used as a substitute. Also, many other vegetables, such as Chinese cabbage, spinach, snow peas, bean sprouts, and so on, can be used instead of broccoli. Although they are not difficult to make, fish cakes do require a little time. You can always make them in two stages: You can either make up the fish paste in advance and refrigerate it for a while, or you can make the paste into fish cakes and then keep them in the refrigerator for 1 or 2 days before cutting them into finger-sized pieces and frying.

INGREDIENTS

2–3 tablespoons dried shrimp

12 ounces skinned and boned haddock fillet, minced

1 teaspoons salt

4 teaspoons cornstarch

3 tablespoons egg white, lightly beaten

6–8 turns white pepper mill

1 1/2 teaspoons minced fresh ginger

3–4 scallions, cut into small rounds

2 long green chiles, seeded and cut into small rounds

7 tablespoons vegetable oil

8–12 ounces broccoli, trimmed and cut into bite-sized pieces

2–3 thin slices fresh ginger, peeled

1 tablespoon Shaoxing wine or medium-dry sherry

SAUCE

1 1/2 teaspoons cornstarch

1 teaspoon thick soy sauce

1–1 1/2 tablespoons oyster sauce

6 tablespoons stock or water

METHOD

■ Rinse the shrimp. Pour over just enough very hot water to cover and leave to stand for 15–20 minutes. Drain. Mince in a food processor or finely chop by hand.

- Prepare the fish paste. Put the minced haddock in a bowl. Add 1 teaspoon of the salt and stir vigorously in the same direction for about 1 minute, until gelatinous in texture. Sprinkle with the cornstarch, add the egg white, then stir until the fish mixture becomes one sticky lump again. Add the pepper, ginger, scallions, and chili and stir to mix well. Divide into 2 equal-sized lumps.

- Blanch the broccoli. Half-fill a wok with water and bring to a boil. Add the remaining 1 teaspoon salt and 1 tablespoon of the oil. Add the broccoli, return to a boil, and continue to cook for 3–4 minutes, or until it is tender yet still has a bite to it. Pour into a colander and refresh under cold running water. Drain.

- Mix the sauce ingredients together and set aside.

- Reheat the wok over a high heat until smoke rises. Add 2 tablespoons oil and swirl it around. Add 1 lump of the fish paste and immediately flatten it with the wok scoop or metal spatula to a circular cake about 7 inches in diameter. Fry for about 30 seconds, lower the heat to medium, and fry for another 60 seconds. Flip over and fry the other side the same way. Both sides of the fish cake should be golden brown but not burned. Remove onto a plate and keep warm nearby.

- Turn up the heat again and add 2 tablespoons of the oil. Fry the remaining lump of fish paste as before. Wash and dry the wok.

- Cut the fish cakes into finger-sized pieces.

- Reheat the wok over a high heat until smoke rises. Add 1 tablespoon oil and swirl it around. Add the ginger slices, stir a few times, then lower the heat to medium. Return the broccoli to the wok and stir until thoroughly hot. Remove to a warm serving dish.

- Reheat the wok until smoke rises. Add the remaining 1 tablespoon oil and swirl it around. Return the fish cakes and flip and turn until very hot again. Splash the wine or sherry around the side of the wok and, when the sizzling dies down, pour in the well-stirred sauce, continuing to stir as the sauce thickens. Remove and arrange on the broccoli. Serve immediately.

NOTE The fish cakes can be made ahead and kept in the refrigerator for up to 2 days.

Whiting with Sweet-and-Sour Sauce

Whiting, an economical but meaty white fish with only a large bone in the center, is rather bland on its own. This vinegary sweet-and-sour sauce is just the answer, for it gives zest to the overall taste, thus upgrading the fish from a homely dish to one fit for entertaining as well.

INGREDIENTS

1 whiting, about 1 1/2 pounds, cleaned with the head left on

3/4–1 teaspoon salt

1 tablespoon fresh ginger juice (see page 25)

Several tablespoons cornstarch

6 tablespoons vegetable oil

2–3 thin slices fresh ginger, peeled

1 inch fresh ginger, peeled and finely chopped

2–3 fresh red or green chiles, cut into small rounds (optional)

3–4 scallions, chopped, white and green parts separated

SAUCE

2 teaspoons cornstarch

4 tablespoons rice vinegar or white wine vinegar

4 tablespoons sugar

3/4 teaspoon salt

2 teaspoons concentrated tomato purée

1 tablespoon thin soy sauce

1 1/2 teaspoons Worcestershire sauce

1 1/2 tablespoons Shaoxing wine or medium-dry sherry

6–7 tablespoons water

METHOD

■ Pat dry the whiting. Make 2 slashes about 1 inch apart across both sides of the thickest part of the fish, but without going all the way to the sides. Rub all over with the salt and ginger juice, including the cavity. Leave to stand for about 15 minutes.

■ Sprinkle over both sides of the fish with a thin layer of cornstarch, shaking off any excess. This helps to keep the skin intact when fried.

■ Mix together the sauce ingredients and set aside.

■ Heat the wok over a high heat until abundant smoke rises. Add 3 tablespoons of the oil and swirl it around the sloping edges as high as possible. Add the ginger slices, fry until burned, then discard. Lower the heat to medium and add the fish. Fry for about 8–9 minutes, tilting the wok back and forth so that the whole length of the fish can be browned evenly. Slip the wok scoop or metal spatula underneath the fish to loosen edges, then carefully turn it over and fry the other side for 8–9 minutes, adding another tablespoon oil around the fish. The fish should be cooked by now. Remove to a serving dish. Wash and dry the wok.

■ Reheat over a high heat until smoke rises. Add the remaining 2 tablespoons oil and swirl it around. Add the chopped ginger, chiles (if using), and white scallions, and stir to release their aroma. Remove the wok from the heat for about 10 seconds. Now add the well-mixed sauce, stir continuously over a gentle heat until it thickens, then boil fiercely. Spoon over the fish and serve immediately.

Sautéed Skate

Skate is available year-round, but you are most likely to find it in a fish store that caters to an Asian market. Skate may also be called ray (as in manta ray), though generally it is the edible members of the family that are skate, when the nonedible members are called ray. The winglike fins are the edible portions and the meat is firm, white, and rather sweet, like scallops.

INGREDIENTS

1 pound skate wing, skinned on one side
1 teaspoon fresh ginger juice (see page 25)
About 3 tablespoons cornstarch
6 tablespoons vegetable oil
1/2 teaspoon salt
2–3 scallions, cut into small rounds
SAUCE
1 1/2 tablespoons thin soy sauce
1/2 teaspoon sugar
2 teaspoons Worcestershire sauce
1 1/2 teaspoons Shaoxing wine or medium-dry sherry
1 tablespoon water

METHOD

■ Pat the fish dry. Rub the ginger juice over the skinless side of the skate and leave to stand for 15 minutes.

■ Coat the skate on both sides with the cornstarch, shaking off any excess.

■ Mix together the sauce ingredients and set aside.

■ Heat the wok over a high heat until smoke rises. Add 4 tablespoons of the oil and swirl it around several times. Add the salt. Lower the skate, skinless side down, into the oil and fry for about 1 minute. Loosening the edges with the wok scoop or a metal spatula, turn the fish over, and fry the other side for about 1 minute. Turn back to the skinless side and continue to sauté over a moderate heat for about 6–7 minutes, or until a thin, golden crust is formed. Turn over and sauté the skinned side for about the same length of time, adding 1 tablespoon of the oil around the fish. The skate should be cooked by now, the flesh flaking easily away from the main bone. Remove to a serving dish.

■ Add the sauce and scallion rounds to the wok and bring to a simmer. Stir in the remaining 1 tablespoon oil, then pour over the skate. Serve immediately.

Wok-Fried Fillet Steak

My father, although his palate was almost exclusively Cantonese, to the extent that he even considered a Peking Duck "foreign," nevertheless enjoyed a beef steak from time to time either at home or in a Western restaurant in Hong Kong. According to him, a steak should be tasty, fragrant, and tender. He introduced this steak to his eight children at a tender age, and we all loved it. I have often cooked it for my son, who is half Chinese and half American, and he, too, loves it.

INGREDIENTS

1 pound flank steak, trimmed and cut into pieces about 1/3–1/2 inch thick

4 1/2 tablespoons vegetable oil

2–3 garlic cloves, crushed but left whole

1 1/2 tablespoons Shaoxing wine or medium-dry sherry

2 medium-sized onions, sliced

Salt

MARINADE

1/4 teaspoon salt

1 tablespoon thick soy sauce

1 teaspoon Worcestershire sauce

8 turns black pepper mill

METHOD

■ Marinate the beef. Smash the beef once with the broadside of a Chinese cleaver or a large knife to loosen the fibers. Add the salt, soy sauce, Worcestershire sauce, and pepper and leave to stand for 30–45 minutes.

■ Heat the wok over a high heat until smoke rises. Add 3 tablespoons of the oil and swirl it around. Add the crushed cloves of garlic, let sizzle and turn brown, releasing its aroma to the oil. Remove the garlic with a perforated spoon and discard.

■ Add the beef to the oil and fry each side for about 15 seconds. Splash in the wine or sherry around the side of the wok. When the sizzling subsides, lower the heat to medium and continue to fry the beef for another 15–45 seconds, depending on how you like it. Remove to a serving platter and keep warm, leaving some oil in the wok.

■ Add the remaining oil and the onions to the wok. Stir and turn over medium high heat for about 1 minute. Season with salt to taste, then remove to the serving platter. Serve immediately.

Lemon Chicken

Refreshing with a lemony taste, this Cantonese dish is very popular in Hong Kong, especially in the summer. The spiced salt is the authentic accompaniment, while the sauce, with its sweet-and-sour appeal to the palates universally, has gained too indomitable a foothold to be ignored.

INGREDIENTS

3 skinned and boned chicken breasts halves, about
    12 ounces

1 large egg yolk

3–4 tablespoons cornstarch

6 tablespoons vegetable oil

Spiced Salt (page 25)

MARINADE

1/2 teaspoon salt

1 teaspoon sugar

6 turns white pepper mill

2 teaspoons Shaoxing wine or medium-dry sherry

2 1/2–3 tablespoons fresh lemon juice

SWEET-AND-SOUR SAUCE

1 1/2 tablespoons lemon juice

1 1/2 tablespoons sugar

1/2 teaspoon salt

1 teaspoon thin soy sauce

1 tablespoon tomato ketchup

1 1/2 teaspoons cornstarch

6 tablespoons water

1 tablespoon vegetable oil

METHOD

■ Cut each chicken breast crossways into thirds. With either the broadside of a cleaver or a mallet, pound the meat 2–3 times to loosen the fibers. Put into a dish.

■ Marinate the chicken. Add the salt, sugar, pepper, wine or sherry, and lemon juice to the chicken. Leave to stand for 1 hour or longer, turning over from time to time and piercing the pieces for better absorption of the marinade.

■ Prepare the sauce. Mix together the lemon juice, sugar, salt, soy sauce, ketchup, cornstarch, and water. Pour into a saucepan (or a second wok) and slowly bring to a simmer, stirring as the sauce thickens. Remove from the heat and stir in the oil.

■ Drain the chicken and put into another dish. Coat with the egg yolk and roll each piece in the cornstarch, shaking off any excess.

■ Heat the wok over a high heat until smoke rises. Add the oil and swirl it around. Add half of the chicken, piece by piece, and do not allow them to stick together. Fry over a medium heat for 1–1 1/2 minutes each side, or until just cooked, crisp and golden on the outside. Remove to a serving plate. Fry the remainder in the same oil.

■ To serve, place both the spiced salt and the sweet-and-sour sauce, reheated at the last moment, on the table and let everybody help themselves.

Chicken Chow-Mein

Here is another chow-mein using chicken instead of ham. With the chicken there is obviously a bit more work involved as the meat needs to be marinated.

INGREDIENTS

8 ounces dried Chinese egg noodles

6 ounces skinned and boneless chicken breast fillet, cut into matchstick-sized pieces

8 tablespoons vegetable oil

4–6 medium-sized Chinese mushrooms, reconstituted (see page 25) and cut into very thin pieces

3 celery ribs, cut diagonally into thin pieces

Pinch of salt

2–3 garlic cloves, finely chopped

3 scallions, cut into 1-inch sections, white and green parts separated

1 tablespoon Shaoxing wine or medium-dry sherry

MARINADE

1/4 teaspoon salt

1/4 teaspoon sugar

2 teaspoons thin soy sauce

6 turns white pepper mill

1–2 teaspoons Shaoxing wine or medium-dry sherry

1 teaspoon cornstarch

1 tablespoon egg white

1 1/2 teaspoons vegetable oil

SAUCE

1/4 teaspoon salt

1 tablespoon thick soy sauce

2 teaspoons cornstarch

3/4 cup water

METHOD

■ Plunge the noodles into a large pot of boiling water, return to a boil, and continue to cook for about 4 minutes, or until *al* dente, separating the noodles with a pair of chopsticks or a fork. Pour into a colander and refresh under cold running water. Drain thoroughly and leave in the colander for 1–2 hours.

■ Marinate the chicken. Add the salt, sugar, soy sauce, pepper, and wine or sherry to the chicken and stir to coat. Sprinkle with the cornstarch, add the egg white, and stir again to coat evenly. Leave to stand for about 20 minutes. Blend in the oil.

■ Heat the wok over a high heat until smoke rises. Add 3 tablespoons of the oil, swirl it around, and wait until smoke rises. Add the noodles, and spread them out so that the surface will be about 8 inches across. Brown the bottom over a medium-high to high heat for 3–4 minutes, peeping to check if they become too brown after the first 2 minutes. Loosen the edges all around and flip the "noodle cake" over, and brown the other side as before, adding 1 tablespoon of the oil around the side of the wok. Transfer to a warm serving dish and keep nearby.

■ Mix together the sauce ingredients and set aside.

■ Add 1 tablespoon oil to the wok and swirl it around. Add the Chinese mushrooms, stir a few times, then add the celery, season with a pinch of salt, and stir for 1–2 minutes over a medium-high heat until thoroughly hot. Remove to a serving dish and keep warm nearby. Wash and dry the wok.

■ Reheat the wok over a high heat until smoke rises. Add 3 tablespoons oil and swirl it around. Add the garlic, let sizzle, then the white scallions, and stir a few times. Add the chicken and, going to the bottom of the wok with the wok scoop or metal spatula, flip and turn for 30–60 seconds, or until the chicken starts to become opaque. Splash the wine or sherry around the side of the wok, continuing to stir as it sizzles. Remove to a dish.

■ Lower the heat, add the well-stirred sauce, stirring as it thickens. Return the celery mixture and chicken to the wok and add the green scallions. Stir to mix, then spoon the ingredients and sauce over the noodles. Serve immediately.

Chicken Thighs with Ham

This recipe is both Chinese and Italian in flavor and technique, inspired by the discovery of packaged skinned and boned chicken thighs in British supermarkets. It is a quick and tasty recipe. If it were made in China, the crimson Jinhua ham from eastern China or Yunnan ham from western China would be used instead of prosciutto. But as neither of these are easy to come by (if ever) in the West, I have been amazed by how reminiscent prosciutto is of the two Chinese hams.

INGREDIENTS

| 8 pieces skinned and boned chicken thigh, about 1 pound |
| 4 thin whole slices prosciutto (Parma ham), halved |
| 1/2 teaspoon salt |
| White pepper to taste |
| 1 1/2 tablespoons egg white, lightly beaten |
| A little cornstarch |
| 3–4 tablespoons vegetable oil |
| 3 tablespoons medium-dry or cream sherry, or Shaoxing wine |

METHOD

■ Cut through the middle of each piece of chicken and place 1 half-piece of prosciutto, folded snugly to fit, on one side. Fold up each chicken thigh again.

■ Sprinkle the chicken thighs with salt and pepper to taste. Coat with the egg white and lightly dust all over with a thin layer of cornstarch, using a sifter or sieve to achieve an even dusting.

■ Heat the wok over a high heat until smoke rises. Add the oil and swirl it around. Add the chicken thighs and brown each side for 1–1 1/2 minutes. Splash in the sherry or Shaoxing wine around the side of the wok and, when the sizzling is less fierce, lower the heat to medium, put on the wok cover, and continue to cook for about 6 minutes. Turn the pieces over and cook, covered, for about another 6 minutes. The chicken thighs should be cooked by now, brown outside but tender inside with most of the juices sealed in, leaving almost pure but fragrant oil around them. Remove from the wok with a slotted spoon and serve immediately.

Ham Chow-Mein

Chow-mein (stir-fried noodles) has become a household name in the West ever since the Chinese emigrants in San Francisco spread the word in the last century. To achieve the best effect, however, one does not stir-fry the noodles but fry them, creating a toasted surface on both sides and a tender soft inside.

INGREDIENTS

6 ounces dried Chinese egg noodles
5 tablespoons vegetable oil
3–4 scallions, cut diagonally into thin slices, white and green parts separated
3–4 celery ribs, cut diagonally into thin slices
4 ounces ham, cut into thin rectangles

SAUCE

1/4 teaspoon salt
1 tablespoon thick soy sauce
2 teaspoons cornstarch
3/4 cup water

METHOD

■ Cook the noodles in a large pot of boiling water for about 4 minutes, or until *al dente*, separating the noodles with a pair of chopsticks or a fork. Pour into a colander and refresh under cold running water. Drain for 1–2 hours.

■ Mix together the sauce ingredients and set aside.

■ Heat the wok over a high heat until smoke rises. Add 3 tablespoons of the oil, swirl it around, and wait until smoke rises. Add the noodles, and spread them out so that the surface will be about 8 inches across. Brown the bottom over a medium-high to high heat for 3–4 minutes, peeping to check if they become too brown after the first 2 minutes. Loosen the edges all around, flip the "noodle cake" over, and brown the other side as before, adding 1 tablespoon of the oil around the side of the wok. Transfer to a warm serving dish.

■ Add the remaining oil to the wok and swirl it around. Add the white scallions and stir a few times. Add the celery and stir for 30–60 seconds. Add the ham and stir until hot. Push the ingredients to the sides of the wok, lower the heat to medium, and pour the well-stirred sauce into the center. As the sauce thickens, stir in the surrounding ingredients, add the green scallions, then spoon the mixture and sauce over the noodles. Serve immediately.

121

Pork Medallions

This typical, modern Chinese family dish reflects the foothold Western influence has gained on the Chinese cuisine in the 20th century. Conversely, the *mélange* of Chinese and Western condiments and the use of onion ("foreign onion" in Chinese) may be regarded as how the Chinese assimilate Western food into their own diet.

INGREDIENTS

12 ounces boneless pork, cut into large chop-size pieces about 1/3 inch thick

2 1/2 teaspoons cornstarch

4 tablespoons vegetable oil

2 medium-sized onions, cut lengthwise into pieces

Salt

6 garlic cloves, left whole

MARINADE

1/4 teaspoon salt

1/4 teaspoon sugar

1 tablespoon thin soy sauce

6 turns white or black pepper mill

1 teaspoon Worcestershire sauce

2 teaspoons Shaoxing wine or medium-dry sherry

SAUCE

1 teaspoon cornstarch

1 teaspoon thin soy sauce

1 teaspoon thick soy sauce

2 teaspoons tomato purée

1 tablespoon hoisin sauce

5 tablespoons water

METHOD

■ Marinate the pork. Add the salt, sugar, soy sauce, pepper, Worcestershire sauce, and wine or sherry to the pork; mix thoroughly. Leave to stand for 1–2 hours, turning the pieces over occasionally.

■ Mix together the sauce ingredients and set aside.

■ Just before you are ready to cook, coat the pork with the cornstarch.

■ Heat the wok over a high heat until smoke rises. Add 1 tablespoon of the oil and swirl it around. Add the onions, season with salt to taste, and turn and toss continuously for about 5 minutes over a low to medium heat, until the onion is partially brown around the edges yet still has a bite to it. Remove and keep warm nearby. Wash and dry the wok.

■ Reheat wok over a high heat until smoke rises. Add 2 tablespoons of the oil and swirl it around several times. Add the garlic, let sizzle for a few seconds, then add half of the pork and fry over a medium heat for about 2–3 minutes. Loosen the edges, turn over, and fry the other side for another 2–3 minutes. The pork should be cooked to a turn by now. Remove to a warm serving dish, leaving the garlic and as much oil as possible behind in the wok.

■ Add the remaining 1 tablespoon oil and swirl it around. Add the remaining pork and fry as before. Discard the burned garlic.

■ Pour into the wok the well-stirred sauce, stir to incorporate the remaining oil, and cook until it thickens, bubbling in a whirlpool. Return the onion to the wok and heat with the sauce until piping hot. Spoon over the pork and serve hot.

Bean Curd with Pork

Each piece of bean curd has an ever-so-thin crust, all the more delightful a contrast to the melting curd consistency inside. The blandness of the bean curd against the well-seasoned pork and sauce is yet another delight to the palate.

INGREDIENTS

4 (1/2-pound) cakes bean curd, quartered
6 ounces boneless pork, 1/2 inch thick, cut into slivers about 1/8 inch wide
4 tablespoons vegetable oil
2 garlic cloves, cut into slivers
2 scallions, cut into 1-inch sections, white and green parts separated
1 tablespoon Shaoxing wine or medium-dry sherry

MARINADE

1/4 teaspoon salt
1/4 teaspoon sugar
2 teaspoons thick soy sauce
4 turns white pepper mill
1 teaspoon Shaoxing wine or medium-dry sherry
3/4 teaspoon cornstarch
2 teaspoons vegetable oil

SAUCE

3/4 teaspoon cornstarch
3 tablespoons water
1 teaspoon thick soy sauce

METHOD

■ Put the bean curd pieces on 2–3 sheets of paper towels to absorb excess water, handling them with care so as not to break them.

■ Marinate the pork. Add the salt, sugar, soy sauce, pepper, wine or sherry, and cornstarch. Mix well to coat. Leave to stand for about 20 minutes. Blend in the oil.

■ Prepare the sauce. Dissolve the cornstarch in the water, add the soy sauce, and stir well.

■ Heat the wok over a high heat until smoke rises. Add the oil, swirl it around, and wait until you see the first sign of smoke. Carefully add half of the bean curd and fry for about 1 minute. Turn each piece over and fry the other side for the same amount of time. The bean curd should not stick to the bottom of the wok. Remove with a perforated metal spoon to a serving plate, draining as much oil back into the wok as possible. Fry the remaining bean curd as before and remove to a serving plate.

■ Add the garlic to the remaining oil in the wok. Let it sizzle for a few seconds, then add the white scallions, and stir a few times. Add the pork and, going to the bottom of the wok with the spatula, heat and toss for about 30 seconds, or until the pork is partially cooked. Splash the wine or sherry around the side of the wok, continuing to stir as it thickens. Add the green scallions, then remove the mixture, and spread over the bean curd. Serve immediately.

Sautéed Stuffed Bean Curd

Stuffing the fragile bean curd may seem like a difficult task, but in fact it isn't, so take heart and try it.

INGREDIENTS

6 cakes firm bean curd, each about 2 1/2 inches square and 1 1/4 inches thick
4 ounces skinned and boned haddock fillet, minced
1/3 teaspoon salt
1 teaspoon cornstarch
1 1/2 tablespoons egg white, lightly beaten
4 turns white pepper mill
1 teaspoon minced fresh ginger
1 ounce ham, minced
6 tablespoons vegetable oil
3 thin slices fresh ginger, peeled
2 teaspoons sesame oil

SAUCE

1 1/2 teaspoons cornstarch dissolved in 1 tablespoon water
2 teaspoons Shaoxing wine or medium-dry sherry
1 teaspoon thick soy sauce
2 tablespoons oyster sauce (or 4 teaspoons thick soy sauce)
6 tablespoons chicken stock

METHOD

■ Steep the bean curd in hot water for about 15 minutes. Drain, handling with care to keep each cake whole. Cut each cake into 3 slices. Lay the rectangular slices flat on paper towels to absorb excess water.

■ Prepare the stuffing. Put the minced haddock in a bowl. Add the salt and stir vigorously in the same direction for about 1 minute, until gelatinous in texture. Sprinkle with cornstarch, add the egg white, then stir until the fish mixture becomes one lump. Add the pepper, ginger, and ham. Stir to mix well.

■ Using a small pointed knife, cut a small rectangle in the center of each slice of bean curd, about 2/3 x 1 inch and 1/4 inch deep. Gently scrape away this layer of bean curd and discard.

■ Into each hollow, put about 1 1/2 teaspoons stuffing and level the stuffing with the surface of the rest of the bean curd.

■ Mix together the sauce ingredients and set aside.

■ Heat the wok over a high heat until smoke rises. Add 4 tablespoons of the oil and swirl it around. Add the ginger, let sizzle until brown, then remove, and discard. Add 6 slices stuffed bean curd, one at a time, stuffing side down, into the oil. Fry over a moderate heat for about 3 minutes, until golden in color. Slipping the wok scoop or metal spatula underneath the bean curd, carefully turn the slices over, one by one. Fry the other side for about 2 minutes. Remove to a serving dish, leaving behind in the wok as much oil as possible.

■ Add 1 tablespoon oil and reheat over a high heat. Add another 6 slices bean curd and fry as before. Repeat until all are done.

■ Lower the heat. Add the well-stirred sauce, and stir until it comes to a boil and thickens. Spoon onto the bean curd. Sprinkle on the sesame oil and serve hot.

127

Sautéed Potato Cakes

Potato is not a staple food for the Chinese, and I grew up eating it occasionally and always as one of the dishes to accompany rice. This particular one, which my aunt made so well for us at home, I find reminiscent of the Swiss rösti.

INGREDIENTS

1 pound potatoes, peeled and cut into large chunks
6 ounces pork with a little fat, finely minced
2 tablespoons hot water
2 tablespoons dried shrimp, rinsed
About 8 tablespoons vegetable oil
2 large shallots, roughly chopped
2 1/2 tablespoons cornstarch

MARINADE

1/4–1/2 teaspoon salt
1/4 teaspoon sugar
2 teaspoons thin soy sauce
6 turns white pepper mill
2 teaspoons Shaoxing wine or medium-dry sherry
3/4 teaspoon cornstarch
1 teaspoon sesame oil

METHOD

■ Boil the potato for about 15 minutes, or until just cooked through. Drain well and mash, but not too finely.

■ Marinate the pork. Add the salt, sugar, soy sauce, pepper, wine or sherry, and cornstarch to the pork, and stir in the same direction to mix thoroughly. Leave to stand for about 15 minutes. Blend in the oil.

■ Pour 2 tablespoons very hot water over the dried shrimp and leave to soak for about 15 minutes. Drain, then chop finely. Mix in with the pork.

■ Heat the wok over a high heat until smoke rises. Add 2 tablespoons of the oil and swirl it around. Add the shallot, and stir about 6 times to release the aroma. Add the pork and, going to the bottom of the wok with the scoop or a metal spatula, turn and flip for 30–45 seconds, or until the pork is barely cooked. Remove and stir into the potato mixture, mixing well. Wash and dry the wok.

■ Stir the cornstarch into the potato mixture. Divide into 8 portions. Flatten them, one by one, between the palms of your hands to make into round cakes, each about 2 1/2 inches across.

■ Reheat the wok over a high heat until smoke rises. Add 2 tablespoons of the oil and swirl it around. Lower the heat to medium and put in 4 potato cakes, taking care not to let them stick to each other. Fry for 3–5 minutes, or until golden brown in color. Carefully turn the cakes over, one by one, and trickle around the edges about 1 tablespoon oil and fry until golden brown. Remove to a serving plate and keep warm nearby.

■ Fry the remainder as before. Serve hot.

Sautéed Pouched Eggs

To be expected, fried eggs can be done in the wok. The Chinese actually do fry their eggs in the wok. Even though they have to be fried individually, the central well of the wok helps to give the fried eggs the perfect round shape—wallet pouches as the Chinese call them—otherwise difficult to achieve in a flat frying pan. The Chinese sometimes eat Pouched Eggs as a side dish when unexpected guests arrive and another dish is needed. A pouched egg is put on top of the rice in the bowl and the yolk, flavored with soy sauce, gives added taste to the rice and makes it more interesting.

INGREDIENTS

About 3 tablespoons vegetable oil
4 large eggs
Salt to taste
1 tablespoon thin or thick soy sauce

METHOD

■ Heat the wok over a high heat until smoke rises. Add 1 tablespoon of the oil and swirl it around. Reduce the heat to medium and add 1 egg to the oil. Fry it for about 1 minute, or until the edges are crinkly and pale golden. Sprinkle with a little salt to taste. Slide the wok scoop or a metal spatula underneath the egg and carefully fold half of the egg over, covering the yolk. Flip the egg over and fry the other side for 10–60 seconds, depending on how runny you like the yolk. Remove to a serving plate and keep warm nearby.

■ Add 1–1 1/2 teaspoons oil to the wok and reheat over a medium heat. Add another egg and fry as before. When all the eggs are done and removed to the serving plate, pour over the soy sauce. Serve immediately.

DEEP-FRYING

▲▲▲▲▲▲▲▲▲▲▲▲▲▲▲▲▲

Deep-frying is a common cooking technique in the cuisines of many different nationalities, but although there are special deep-fryers in which to do the job, the Chinese have always used their versatile woks. Just as with steaming, the wok must sit securely on its stand on top of the burner before oil is poured in, filling about halfway up the sides. If the level of oil comes too far up, common sense tells you that it may easily spill over when food is added, causing a fire hazard and possible skin burns.

When it comes to heating the oil, there are several ways to test its readiness. A good old Chinese way is to throw in a small round of green scallion; if it sizzles fiercely on the surface, the oil is hot enough. A Western counterpart is the stale bread cube; the hotter the oil, the shorter length of time it takes for the cube to brown. The most reliable method, especially for an inexperienced cook, is to use a special deep-frying thermometer. I use this last method whenever I deep-fry, and I have detailed the correct temperatures for all the recipes in this section.

To deep-fry Chinese food successfully in the wok, you must have a perforated spoon or, better still, a large strainer in place of the Western frying basket. If possible, use a long pair of bamboo chopsticks with which to move the food around while it is cooking, in order to prevent pieces sticking together, although you can always use a wooden spoon.

Always, when food is removed from the oil, put it on some of our wonderful paper towels to absorb any excess grease.

What is the desired effect of deep-fried food, you may well ask? It should be golden in color, the batter crisp to the bite while the ingredients inside are juicy and tender. To achieve this, a very quick second immersion in the hot oil will give an extra crispy result.

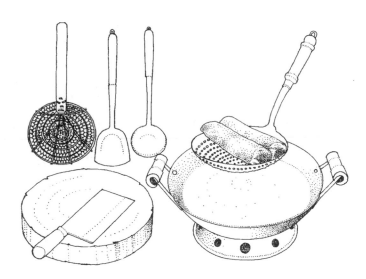

Shrimp Toasts

These are not only delicious but also fun to make. What is important is to make a very light shrimp paste. This recipe makes 32 pieces.

INGREDIENTS

1 pound medium-sized raw shrimp in the shell, fresh or frozen
1 teaspoon salt
1/4 teaspoon sugar
1 teaspoon cornstarch
1 egg white
2 1/2–3 ounces pork fat, minced
6–8 water chestnuts, fresh or canned, peeled and minced
8–9 pieces one-day-old white bread without crust
White sesame seeds
Vegetable oil for deep-frying
Chili sauce

METHOD

■ If frozen shrimp are used, defrost thoroughly. Shell and devein. Pat dry. Mince either by hand or in a food processor. Transfer to a large bowl.

■ Prepare the shrimp paste. Add the salt and sugar to the minced shrimp and stir in the same direction until it is difficult to continue. Sprinkle with the cornstarch, add the egg white, and stir again vigorously for 1–2 minutes, or until the paste is light and fluffy in texture. Add the pork fat and water chestnut and stir to mix well. Leave in the refrigerator, covered, for 30 minutes.

■ Cut each piece of bread into 4 triangles, about 2 x 2 x 2 1/2 inches. With a knife, spread all over the top of each triangle of bread some shrimp paste, shaping it into a slightly sloping mound to give an attractive appearance. Leave the sides of the bread clean but smear a tiny bit of paste over the corners to stick the paste to the bread. Roll the shrimp paste side of the triangles on the sesame seeds.

■ Half-fill the wok with oil and heat over a high heat until it reaches 350° F or until a cube of stale bread browns in about 60 seconds. Add the triangles, paste side down, 8–10 at a time, or as many as can float freely, and deep-fry for about

1 1/2 minutes, or until the corners take on color. Turn over the triangles. As soon as the bread is golden brown, remove and drain on paper towels.

■ Reheat the oil to the same temperature and deep-fry the remainder as before. Remove the toasts to a serving platter. Serve with the chili sauce dip.

NOTE Deep-fried shrimp toasts can be frozen. Also, if you are in a great hurry, instead of cutting a piece of bread into triangles, simply spread the shrimp paste onto the whole piece. Cut into strips or triangles after frying.

Phoenix Rolls

These rolls undoubtedly belong to the realm of Chinese *haute cuisine*, involving as they do many steps and techniques. The end result is one of grand simplicity, well deserving the accolade of the name "phoenix," an emblem of royalty and beauty in traditional China. This recipe serves 4 for lunch with a salad or 8–12 as a first course.

INGREDIENTS

4 scallions, 7 1/2–8 inches long
2 egg whites, lightly beaten
2 egg yolks
Cornstarch
Vegetable oil for deep-frying

SHRIMP PASTE

1 pound medium-sized raw shrimp in the shell, fresh or frozen
1 teaspoon salt
1 teaspoon cornstarch
1 egg white
2 1/2–3 ounces pork fat (lard), minced
6–8 water chestnuts, fresh or canned, peeled and minced

CRÊPES

4 large eggs
4 teaspoons cornstarch
4 teaspoons water
Salt
2 tablespoons vegetable oil

METHOD

■ Prepare the shrimp paste. If frozen shrimp are used, defrost thoroughly. Shell and devein the shrimp. Pat dry. Mince either by hand or in a food processor. Transfer to a large bowl.

■ Add the salt and stir in the same direction until it is difficult to continue. Sprinkle with the cornstarch, add the egg whites and stir again vigorously for 1–2 minutes, or until the paste is light and fluffy in texture. Add the pork fat and water chestnuts and stir well to mix. Leave in the refrigerator, covered, for 30 minutes or longer.

■ Meanwhile prepare the crêpes. Beat 1 egg lightly, then 1 teaspoon of the cornstarch dissolved in 1 teaspoon water. Season with salt. Heat an 8-inch flat frying pan, preferably nonstick, over a moderate heat until hot. Add 1 tablespoon oil, swirl it around to reach the sides, then pour off half of it. Pour in the egg and tip the pan making sure it reaches the edges in one even layer. Fry over a low heat until set, but not brown. Carefully loosening the edges with a metal spatula, flip the crêpe over, and fry the other side until set. Remove to a flat plate or surface and let cool.

■ Repeat this process until 4 crêpes are made.

■ Divide the shrimp paste into 4 equal portions. Using your fingers, spread 1 portion evenly over half of the crêpe, stopping just short of the circular edge. Place 1 scallion across the center of the crêpe next to the shrimp paste. Again, using your fingers (or a pastry brush), smear egg white on the other half of the crêpe, going to the circular edge as well.

■ Pick up the half with shrimp paste and roll away from your body into a sausage—the Phoenix Roll. The egg white on the other half will seal the roll.

■ Repeat until all 4 rolls are done.

■ Put the rolls, 2 at a time, onto a lightly oiled heatproof dish and steam them in the wok (see page 43) for 10–12 minutes, until the shrimp paste is cooked. Remove from the dish and let cool for a few minutes. Wash and dry the wok.

■ Brush each roll with egg yolk, then roll, one by one, over the cornstarch until evenly coated. Shake off any excess, if necessary.

■ Half-fill the wok with oil and heat over a high heat until it reaches the temperature of 350° F, or until a cube of stale bread browns in about 60 seconds. Lower the rolls into the oil and deep-fry them for about 4 minutes, or until golden in color, turning them over from time to time. Remove with a large perforated strainer, then immerse them in the oil again for about 10–20 seconds to crisp a second time. Remove and put on paper towels.

■ If the Phoenix Rolls are to be served as a first course or hors d'oeuvres, place them on a platter and cut diagonally into pieces about 1 inch wide. Chili and Worcestershire sauces can be used as dips.

Smoked Halibut or Turbot

The technique of preparing this dish is adapted from the well-known Cantonese dish called Smoked Pomfret. While pomfret, a fish of subtle taste and texture, is easily available in South China, Southeast Asia, and India, it is never seen fresh in Europe and North America. But cod, halibut, and turbot, all available on both sides of the Atlantic Ocean, can be used successfully as substitutes. Compared to halibut and turbot, cod steaks are much more economical, while their taste and texture, unfortunately, are just as much less interesting.

INGREDIENTS

2–3 halibut or turbot steaks, about 1 1/4 pounds, each 1/2 inch thick

4–5 large leaves iceberg lettuce, cut into very thin strips

3 red tomatoes, cut into thin slices

Oil for deep-frying

2 tablespoons sugar

1 tablespoon black tea leaves (Chinese or Indian)

Mayonnaise

SPICED LIQUID

1 tablespoon vegetable oil

1 1/2 inches fresh ginger, peeled and crushed

2 scallions, halved crossways

1 cup water

1 teaspoon salt

1 tablespoon thin soy sauce

1/2 teaspoon ground cinnamon or five-spice powder

1 tablespoon Shaoxing wine or medium-dry sherry

METHOD

■ Prepare the spiced liquid. Heat the wok over high heat until smoke rises. Add the oil and swirl it around. Add the ginger and scallions and stir to release their aroma. Add the water and season with the salt, soy sauce, and cinnamon or five-spice powder. Bring to a boil, then continue to boil for 10–15 minutes, reducing the water to about 1 cup. Pour the mixture into a shallow bowl and let cool to room temperature. Add the wine or sherry.

■ Pat dry the fish. Add to the spiced liquid, which should almost or just cover the fish. Leave to stand for 3 hours, turning over from time to time and piercing the flesh with a sharp knife for better absorption of the soaking liquid.

■ About 15–30 minutes before deep-frying them, lift the fish out of the liquid and put onto a wire rack to dry off excess moisture. Discard the spiced liquid.

■ Spread the lettuce in the middle of a serving dish and arrange the tomato slices around it. Put into the refrigerator to chill until the fish is ready to be served.

■ Half-fill the wok with oil and heat to a temperature of 375–400° F, or until a cube of stale bread foams fiercely immediately. Carefully lower the fish into the oil and deep-fry for 8–10 minutes, until light brown in color, turning them over once. Remove with a large hand strainer or perforated spoon and put onto paper towels.

■ Empty the oil into a container for another use. Leave the wok oily and unwashed.

■ Sprinkle the sugar into the center of the wok, then sprinkle the tea leaves on top. Transfer the fish to a latticed rack (wire or bamboo) that is fitted into the wok above the sugar and tea, leaving a gap of 1/2–1 inch. Put on the wok lid. Turn on a high heat to produce smoke by melting the sugar and burning the tea leaves. Smoke the fish for 3–5 minutes from the time you see smoke escaping from the wok lid. Remove from the heat. (The layer of burned sugar and tea can be easily removed from the oiled wok.)

■ Place the fish on top of the lettuce in the serving plate. Serve either hot or cold. Use the mayonnaise as a dip.

Lemon Sole with Sweet-and-Sour Sauce

The delicate texture of the lemon sole is well complemented by this very light batter.

INGREDIENTS

About 1 1/2 pounds lemon sole fillets
Vegetable oil for deep-frying
Batter
1 cup self-raising flour
1 large egg
9 tablespoons iced water
1/2 teaspoon salt
1 tablespoon vegetable oil
SAUCE
3–4 teaspoons cornstarch
1 cup water
3 tablespoons rice or white wine vinegar
3–3 1/2 tablespoons sugar
1/2 teaspoon salt
2 teaspoons thin soy sauce
1 teaspoon Worcestershire sauce
1 tablespoon tomato ketchup
1 tablespoon vegetable oil

METHOD

■ Prepare the batter. Sift the flour into a mixing bowl and stir in the egg. Add the water gradually, stirring to blend into a smooth batter, the consistency of cream. Add the salt. Leave to stand for 20–30 minutes, then blend in the oil to make it smoother.

■ Prepare the sauce. Dissolve the cornstarch in about 2 tablespoons of the water; add the vinegar, sugar, salt, soy sauce, Worcestershire sauce, and ketchup. Stir in the remaining water. Pour into a saucepan (or a second wok) and cook over medium heat until the sauce thickens, stirring to ensure that it does not become lumpy. Remove from the heat and blend in the oil. Keep nearby.

■ Pat dry the lemon sole fillets. Halve lengthwise, then cut each half crossways into 2–3 pieces.

■ Half-fill the wok with oil and heat over a high heat until it reaches a temperature of 375° F, or until a cube of stale bread browns in about 50 seconds. In the meantime, add half of the fish to the batter to coat. Using a pair of bamboo chopsticks or tongs, lift the fish, piece by piece, and put into the oil to deep-fry for about 1 minute, or until pale golden. (When the last piece goes into the oil, the first will be almost ready to come out.) Remove onto paper towels to drain. Coat and deep-fry the remaining fish as before.

■ Reheat the oil to the same temperature. Add all the fish to deep-fry a second time for about 30 seconds, crisping the batter to a turn. Remove with a large hand strainer or perforated disc onto paper towels, then transfer to a serving plate.

■ Reheat the sauce, pour over the fish, and serve immediately. (The sauce can also be served in a bowl for individuals to use as a dip.)

Deep-Fried Spareribs

These spareribs have a hot, sweet-and-sour sauce.

INGREDIENTS

1 1/2 pounds pork spareribs, cut into 2-inch pieces
2–2 1/2 tablespoons cornstarch
Oil for deep-frying
2 large garlic cloves, lightly crushed
4 tomatoes, cut into thin slices

MARINADE

1/2 teaspoon salt
1/2 teaspoon sugar
1 tablespoon thin soy sauce
2 teaspoons Shaoxing wine or medium-dry sherry

SAUCE

1 1/2 teaspoons cornstarch
5 tablespoons water
2 tablespoons Chinese red vinegar or red wine vinegar
2 tablespoons sugar
1 tablespoon chili sauce
1/4 teaspoon salt

METHOD

■ Remove excess fat from the ribs, if any. (The fat, if rendered down, makes the best lard.) Pat dry the spareribs.

■ Marinate the spareribs. Add the salt, sugar, soy sauce, and wine or sherry to the spareribs and mix thoroughly. Leave to stand for 3–4 hours, turning them over occasionally. The marinade should be all absorbed at the end of the marinating time.

■ Mix together the sauce ingredients and set aside.

■ Just before you are ready to cook, sprinkle the ribs with the cornstarch and mix to coat well.

■ Half-fill the wok with oil and heat to 300° F, or until a cube of stale bread foams slowly. Carefully add all the spareribs, lowering the heat to maintain a temperature of between 200–250° F, or until only tiny whirlpools are seen on the surface of the oil. Steep the spareribs, the thin pieces for about 10 minutes and the thick pieces for 15 minutes, or until they are just cooked, separating them with a long pair of bamboo chopsticks or a wooden spoon. Remove with a large hand strainer or perforated spoon and drain on paper towels. This step can be done several hours ahead.

■ Reheat the oil to a temperature of 350–375° F. Return the spareribs to the wok and deep-fry for 1–2 minutes to crisp the outside. Remove and drain on paper towels. Empty the oil into a container and save for another use. Wash and dry the wok.

■ Reheat the wok over a high heat until smoke rises. Add 1 tablespoon oil and swirl it around. Add the garlic, let sizzle and take on color, releasing the aroma. Remove from the heat and let the oil cook for 20–30 seconds. Add the well-stirred sauce and bring to a boil over a gentle heat, stirring as it thickens. Discard the garlic.

■ Return the spareribs to the wok and mix thoroughly with the sauce. Remove to a serving dish. Arrange the tomato on either side. Serve immediately.

Crispy Skin Bean Curd

Shatin in the New Territory of Hong Kong has always been famous for this dish; on the weekends, people throng there to eat it. I used to be in awe of such a gastronomic feat—a very light and crispy skin covering a velvet smooth and soft curd in the center—until I determined to find out how to prepare it.

INGREDIENTS

4 cakes bean curd, each usually about 2 1/2 inches square and 1 1/4 inches thick
Oil for deep-frying
Spiced Salt (see page 25)
BATTER
1/2 cup all-purpose flour
2 tablespoons cornstarch
3/4 teaspoon baking powder
About 1/2 cup iced water
1 teaspoon salt
2 tablespoons vegetable oil

METHOD

■ Prepare the batter. Sift the flour, cornstarch, and baking powder into a fairly wide-bottomed mixing bowl. Add the water gradually, stirring vigorously to mix into a very smooth and thin batter. Test by lifting a fork from the bottom of the bowl; if the batter runs down in a continuous stream, breaking into drops only at the end, it is of the right consistency. Stir in the salt and leave to stand in the refrigerator for 30 minutes or longer. Blend in the oil.

■ Cut each bean curd square into 3 rectangular pieces. Dab off any excess water with paper towels, handling with care.

■ Half-fill the wok with oil. Heat to a temperature of 375–400° F, or until a cube of stale bread foams very fast in the oil.

■ When the oil is almost ready, dip the bean curd, 2–3 pieces at a time, into the batter to coat thoroughly. Using either a pair of chopsticks or a perforated spoon, gently lift them, 1 piece at a time, from the batter (let some of the excess batter drip back into the bowl) and into the oil, and deep-fry for 3–4 minutes, or until golden in color. Make sure the pieces float freely in the oil. Remove the individual pieces as soon as they are ready with a perforated spoon and put on paper towels.

■ Gently plunge all the bean curd pieces together into the oil again and deep-fry a second time to crisp for 20–30 seconds. Remove together and put onto paper towels.

■ Place on a serving plate and serve immediately. The spiced salt is used as a dip to individual taste.

BRAISING

▲▲▲▲▲▲▲▲▲▲▲▲▲▲▲▲▲▲▲

Braising food the Chinese way is not all that different from doing it the Western way, except in the use of seasoning and herbs. In the West, and in most other cuisines, very many different herbs and seasonings are used, whereas the Chinese very often just use star anise, a few Sichuan peppercorns, some thick soy sauce, and a little rice wine or sherry. Through this grand simplicity we achieve the most sophisticated results.

Basically, the method consists of browning the main ingredient in a little fat, then cooking it in a fair amount of liquid for a long time until it is tender and richly seasoned by the sauce. A deep, heavy pot is the ideal utensil for this kind of cooking as a rule, yet the wok, complete with its spacious plateau dome cover, can be used to turn out deliciously braised dishes. It is especially suitable if the braising process is not an overly lengthy one and more in the pot-roast fashion (see Wok-Roasted Chicken on page 151) than it is for a stew with plenty of gravy.

When it comes to vegetables, sometimes there is only a fine line between braising and stir-frying. For example, Chinese leaves can be thinly sliced and stir-fried very quickly, but if they are left in large chunks, the wok lid put on and the heat lowered, the leaves will take at least 20 minutes to become tender—and thus become a braised dish.

As in steaming, the wok lid plays an important role and should fit tightly to the sloping sides of the wok. The amount of liquid in which the food is cooked should also be checked from time to time and replenished if need be.

Braised Beef Steaks

A family dish that will go well not only with rice, but also with potato and pasta.

INGREDIENTS

2 tablespoons vegetable oil
2 large garlic cloves, crushed but kept whole
8–10 segments star anise
1 inch cinnamon, finely crushed
6 beef shanks, each about 6 ounces and 3/4 inch thick
2 tablespoons Shaoxing wine or medium-dry sherry
1 tablespoon thin soy sauce
1 tablespoon thick soy sauce
1/2 teaspoon salt
1 teaspoon sugar
1 cup unseasoned beef or chicken stock
2 3/4 teaspoons cornstarch dissolved in 3 tablespoons water

METHOD

■ Heat the wok over a high heat until smoke rises. Add the oil and swirl it around. Add the garlic, let sizzle and take on color. Adjusting the heat to medium, add the star anise and cinnamon and stir a few times. Add the steaks and brown for about 2 minutes on each side. Pour in the Shaoxing wine or sherry, turning up the heat to reduce it by half.

■ Reduce the heat again and sit the wok on its stand. Add the soy sauces, salt, sugar, and the stock. Simmer for about 2 3/4–3 hours, so gently that at the end of the cooking time there will still be about 1 cup sauce in the wok with the shanks remaining whole. Turn the shanks over at the end of every hour and, if necessary, add more stock or water.

■ Remove the meat to a serving platter and keep warm nearby. Pass the sauce through a sieve and discard the solids. Return the sauce to the wok, add the well-stirred dissolved cornstarch, and bring to a simmer over a gentle heat, stirring, until it thickens. Pour the sauce over the steaks or serve it separately.

Madame So's Wok-Roasted Chicken

Even though my mother, So Lam Mo-yin, is more interested in fundamentalist Christianity than food, she nevertheless produces a superb chicken dish that all her children unanimously vote to be superior to any other of its kind they have tasted anywhere. Whenever we go home to Hong Kong to visit her, she will cook this dish for us to satisfy our deprived taste buds. Recently, upon my request, she wrote down the procedures for me in meticulous detail, which I have rendered from Chinese into English below.

INGREDIENTS

1 chicken, 2 3/4–3 pounds
1 3/4 teaspoons salt
10 scallions, trimmed
5 tablespoons vegetable oil
2 tablespoons cloud ears, reconstituted (see page 25) and broken into pieces
6 medium-sized dried Chinese mushrooms, reconstituted and cut into very thin slices
1/3 ounce golden needles, reconstituted
2 tablespoons water
3 large garlic cloves, crushed but left whole
3 thick slices fresh ginger, peeled
8 segments (1 whole) star anise
1/2 teaspoon Sichuan peppercorns
8 tablespoons water

SAUCE

4 tablespoons thick soy sauce
1 1/2 teaspoons brown sugar
1 tablespoon Shaoxing wine or medium-dry sherry

METHOD

■ Pat dry the chicken. Rub 1 1/2 teaspoons of the salt all over the skin and in the cavity of the chicken and leave to stand for 30–40 minutes.

■ Meanwhile, plunge the scallions into a wok half-filled with boiling water. Blanch for about 10 seconds to make them pliable. Pour into a colander and refresh them with cold water. Drain.

■ Make a knot in each of the scallions. Set aside.

■ Mix together the sauce ingredients and set aside.

■ Prepare the stuffing. Heat the wok over a high heat until smoke rises. Add 2 tablespoons of the oil and swirl it around. Add the scallion loops, stir several times, then add the cloud ears and stir. Add the mushrooms and stir. Then add the golden needles and continue to stir for another 30 seconds. Sprinkle with 2 tablespoons of water, season with the remaining 1/4 teaspoon salt, and cook, covered, for about 2 minutes, or until the water is absorbed. Remove the stuffing onto a plate. Wash and dry the wok.

■ Reheat the wok over a high heat until smoke rises. Add the remaining 3 tablespoons oil and swirl it around. Add the garlic and stir. Add the ginger and stir. Add the star anise and Sichuan peppercorns. Lower the chicken into the oil to brown over a medium heat for 4–5 minutes, turning from breast to back and side to side and taking care not to burn the condiments. Pour over the well-stirred sauce and bring to a simmer. Remove the wok from the heat.

■ Place the stuffing into the cavity of the chicken. (This can be done either by removing the chicken to a plate or leaving it in the wok.)

■ Stand the chicken on its side in the wok. Add 4 tablespoons water and simmer fast, covered tightly, over a moderate heat for 20–25 minutes. Remove the lid, ladle the sauce over the chicken several times, turn it to stand on its other side. Add another 4 tablespoons water and continue to cook, covered, for another 20–25 minutes. Insert a chopstick into the thickest part of the thigh; if the juice which oozes out is clear, the chicken is cooked.

■ To serve it Chinese style, remove the chicken onto a chopping board. Scoop out the stuffing and place it on a serving platter. Carve the chicken through the bones into 1-inch pieces and arrange them over the stuffing. Pour the sauce, reheated to a simmer, over the chicken. Alternatively, the chicken can be carved like a Western-style oven-roasted chicken, and the stuffing and sauce served separately.

Braised Chicken Wings

Chicken wings (for that matter duck's wings as well) which are not highly regarded in the West and hence inexpensive, are a Chinese gourmet's delight. Try this recipe, but remember not to chop off the pinions.

INGREDIENTS

2 pounds or 12 chicken wings
1/2 teaspoon salt
10 turns white pepper mill
2–2 1/2 tablespoons vegetable oil
3 garlic cloves, crushed
3 slices fresh ginger, each about 1/4 inch thick, peeled and bruised
3 scallions, cut into 2-inch sections, white and green parts separated
8 segments (1 whole) star anise
1 1/2 inches cinnamon stick, crushed into bits
1 tablespoon Shaoxing wine or medium-dry sherry

SAUCE

3 1/2 tablespoons thick soy sauce or 2 tablespoons thick soy and 2 tablespoons oyster sauce
4 tablespoons water
1 teaspoon sugar

METHOD

■ Pat dry the chicken wings. Sprinkle over with the salt and pepper and leave to stand for about 30 minutes.

■ Mix together the sauce ingredients and set aside.

■ Heat the wok over a high heat until smoke rises. Add the oil and swirl it around. Add the garlic and stir, then add the ginger and white scallions and stir to release their aroma. Add the star anise and cinnamon and stir a few more times, adjusting the heat so as not to burn the condiments. Add the chicken wings to brown gently with the condiments for about 5 minutes, turning them over frequently with the wok scoop or metal spatula. Splash in the wine or sherry around the side of the wok. When the sizzling subsides, pour in the well-stirred sauce.

■ Bring the sauce to a boil. Place the lid on the wok and continue to cook over a low to medium heat for 30 minutes, if you like the meat to be tender but firm, or for 60 minutes if you prefer it to be falling off the bones. In either case, turn the wings over halfway through the cooking time for even cooking and coloring. It may be necessary to add 3–4 tablespoons water if you choose the longer cooking period.

• Remove the lid. Turn up the heat and add the green scallions. Spoon the sauce in the wok over the wings continuously for 1–2 minutes. This reducing process enriches the taste and gives the sauce a slight glazing effect. Remove to a serving platter and serve hot.

NOTE The chicken wings are also delicious served cold.

Duck with Pearl Onions

Covered with a lid, the wok becomes an effective casserole for slow cooking. This braised duck, with its tender yet firm-textured meat, is evocative of roast duck.

INGREDIENTS

1 oven-ready duck, about 4 1/2 pounds
Thick soy sauce
5 tablespoons vegetable oil
12–18 pearl onions
3 tablespoons Shaoxing wine or medium-dry sherry
1 teaspoon salt
1 teaspoon brown sugar
1 cup chicken stock
3 tablespoons thick soy sauce
2 whole star anise or 16 segments
2 inches cinnamon stick, broken up
1 cup water

METHOD

■ Pour a kettle of boiling water all over the duck to scald the skin, which will shrink instantly and become glossy. This helps to keep the shape of the duck. Wipe off excess water. While the skin is still warm, brush all over with thick soy sauce to color it.

■ Heat a wok over high heat until smoke rises. Add the oil and swirl it around. Lower the duck into the oil to brown, breast side down first, then turn over and sideways. Fry for 4–5 minutes, until the skin takes on color. Remove the duck.

■ Add the whole onions to the oil and fry over a high heat for 1–2 minutes. Lift to a plate with a perforated spoon. Remove most of the oil (which can be saved to cook vegetables like cabbage or cauliflower).

■ Return the duck to the wok. Add the wine or sherry, salt, sugar, chicken stock, 3 tablespoons thick soy sauce, star anise, and cinnamon. Add also about 1 cup water and bring to a boil. Reduce the heat, cover with the wok lid, and simmer for about 1 1/2 hours. Add the onions around the duck, replenish with a little more water or stock, and continue to simmer, covered, for another hour.

■ Remove the onions and keep warm nearby. Turn up the heat to reduce the sauce, spooning it over the duck repeatedly until the sauce becomes thicker and glazed. Alternatively, thicken the sauce with cornstarch (about 4 teaspoons cornstarch dissolved in 2 tablespoons water for every 1 cup sauce).

■ Remove the duck to a serving platter and arrange the onions around it. Carve it your usual way, or break it up into chunks with chopsticks.

Eggplant with Bacon

The spongy flesh of eggplant is inclined to absorb too much cooking fat, and the result can be a greasy dish, if one is not careful. A little vinegar, however, cuts the grease, and the sweet red pepper enlivens the color and gives this earthy dish harmony in flavor.

INGREDIENTS

4 tablespoons vegetable oil
4 ounces streaky bacon slices, cut into pieces
2–3 garlic cloves, crushed
3–4 scallions, cut into 2-inch sections, white and green parts separated
1 1/4 pounds eggplant, trimmed and cut into fairly large pieces
1/2 teaspoon salt
1 teaspoon sugar
1 tablespoon Shaoxing wine or medium-dry sherry
1 tablespoon rice or white wine vinegar
1 tablespoon thin soy sauce
1/2 cup clear stock or water
1 large red pepper, about 8 ounces, seeded and roughly chopped

METHOD

■ Heat the wok over a high heat until smoke rises. Add 2 tablespoons of the oil and swirl it around. Add the bacon and stir for about 1 minute, until partially cooked and fragrant.

■ Add the remaining 2 tablespoons oil. Add the garlic and white scallions and stir to release their aroma. Add the eggplant and, going to the bottom of the wok with the wok scoop or a metal spatula, turn and toss for about 1 minute to brown the pieces. Lower the heat. Add the salt, sugar, wine or sherry, vinegar, soy sauce, and stock or water. Stir to mix. Put on the wok cover and continue to cook over a low heat for about 45 minutes or until the eggplant is tender and the spongy flesh impregnated with the sauce. Check for liquid at half time and carefully turn the pieces over a few times. (The eggplant can be prepared up to this point several hours ahead.)

■ Mix in the red pepper and continue to cook, covered, for 10 more minutes. Add the green scallions, mix, then spoon onto a serving dish and serve hot.

NOTE Vegetarians can simply omit the bacon and add instead 1 extra tablespoon oil at the beginning and perhaps 1–2 teaspoons sesame oil at the end as well.

REFERENCES

References for drawings of excavated Chinese cooking pots as shown on page 15.

1. Ma Jianxi. "Brief Report on the Excavations of the Warring States and Western Han Tombs of Yao Xian, Shaanxi Province," *Kaogu* (*Archeology*) 1959, No. 3, p. 149; Plate IV, fig. 5.
2. Jiangxi Provincial Museum. "The Eastern Han and Eastern Wu Tombs at Nanchang in Jiangxi Province," *Kaogu* (*Archeology*) 1978, No. 3, pp. 161–62; Plate V, fig. 6.
3. Li Zhengguang. "Excavations of Ancient Cemeteries at Shahu Qiao in Changsha," *Kaogu Xuebao* (*The Chinese Journal of Archaeology*) 1957, No. 4, p. 62; Plate XII, fig. 10.
4. The Nanjing Museum and the Municipal Museum of Yangzhou. "The Han Dynasty Wooden-chambered Tomb at Qilidian, Yangzhou, Jiangsu," *Kaogu* (*Archeology*) 1962, No. 8, p. 402; Plate V, fig. 3.
5. Wang Zengxin. "The Jin and Yuan Sites in Chenghou Village, Liaoning Province," *Kaogu* (*Archeology*) 1960, No. 2, p. 43; Plate V, fig. 4
6. Tian Jingdong. "The Discovery of Yuan Artefacts Stored in a Cellar in Liangxiang near Beijing (Peking)," *Kaogu* (*Archeology*) 1972, No. 2, pp. 33–34.
7. Su Tianjun. "The Liao and Jin Iron Implements Unearthed at Beijing," *Kaogu* (*Archeology*) 1963, No. 3, pp. 140–44.

Reference books:

Chang, K. C. ed. *Food in Chinese Culture: Anthropological and Historical Perspectives* (Yale University Press, 1978).

Needham, Joseph. *The Development of Iron and Steel Technology in China* (W. Heffer & Sons Limited, 1964).

Song Yingxing. *Tian Gong Kai Wu* (The Exploitation of the Works of Nature) (1637).

INDEX

COOKBOOKS BY THE CROSSING PRESS

Homestyle Cooking Series

Homestyle Mexican Cooking

By Lourdes Nichols

This tantalizing collection of over 180 authentic recipes from Mexican cuisine includes meat and poultry dishes and recipes for rice dishes, vegetables, salads, desserts, and drinks.

$16.95 • Paper • ISBN 0-89594-861-3

Homestyle Middle Eastern Cooking

By Pat Chapman

This collection of authentic recipes features spicy regional dishes selected from hundreds of recipes the author collected on his travels throughout the Middle East.

$16.95 • Paper • ISBN 0-89594-860-5

Homestyle Thai and Indonesian Cooking

By Sri Owen

Sri Owen offers authentic recipes for satés, curries, fragrant rice dishes, spicy vegetables, and snacks and sweets. Includes adaptations using Western ingredients.

$16.95 • Paper • ISBN 0-89594-859-1

Homestyle Italian Cooking

By Lori Carangelo

These wonderful dishes use fresh ingredients, carefully prepared to bring out the special flavors of the best, homestyle Italian cooking.

$16.95 • Paper • ISBN 0-89594-867-2

Global Grilling
Sizzling Recipes from Around the World
By Jay Solomon

Over 100 recipes from around the world, including healthful vegetarian dishes and an appealing array of marinades, spice rubs, and basting sauces.

"A good value and a valuable addition to active cookery collections." —*Booklist*

$10.95 • Paper • ISBN 0-89594-666-1

Global Kitchen
Meat and Vegetarian Recipes from Africa, Asia and Latin America for Western Kitchens
By Troth Wells

Celebrates the wholesome food cooked and eaten by everyday people in Asia, the Middle East, Africa and Latin America.

$16.95 • Paper • ISBN 0-89594-753-6

The World in Your Kitchen
Vegetarian Recipes from Africa, Asia and Latin America
By Troth Wells
Foreword by Glenda Jackson

"Highlights the rich diversity of foods from around the world." —*Vegetarian Gourmet*

$16.95 • Paper • ISBN 0-89594-577-0

International Vegetarian Cooking
by Judy Ridgway

This collection of more than 400 new vegetarian dishes adapted from the world's most popular cuisines also outlines dietary guidelines, offers tips for successful menu planning, gives time-saving suggestions, and provides ideas for special occasions.

$14.95 • Paper • ISBN 0-89594-854-0

Island Cooking
Recipes from the Caribbean
By Dunstan Harris

A calypsonian blend of European, African, Indian, Chinese and Native American influences, Caribbean cooking is spicy and satisfying. These recipes represent the cultures and ethnic blends found in the Caribbean.

$10.95 • Paper • ISBN 0-89594-400-6

Japanese Vegetarian Cooking
From Simple Soups to Sushi
By Patricia Richfield

Easy-to-follow directions, information on techniques, plus a glossary of Japanese ingredients make this is a must-have cookbook for all Japanese food fans. Vegans and vegetarians will also welcome it as an opportunity to expand their menus.

$14.95 • Paper • ISBN 0-89594-805-2

Low-Fat Vegetarian Cooking
By Sue Kreitzman

Adapting popular vegetarian dishes from the cuisines of the world, Master chef Sue Kreitzman has created more than 100 new low-fat or non-fat dishes for vegetarians and anyone wanting to reduce the fat in their diets.

$14.95 • Paper • ISBN 0-89594-834-6

Indian Cuisine

From Bengal to Punjab
The Cuisines of India

By Smita Chandra

Homestyle Indian food featuring recipes and techniques handed down through generations of the author's family; breads, barbeque fare, spice blends and chutneys.

$12.95 • Paper • ISBN 0-89594-509-6

The Spice Box
Vegetarian Indian Cookbook

By Manju Shivraj Singh

"An imaginative collection of recipes that will be of interest to the seasoned chef of Indian cuisine. A cookbook well suited to the adventurous vegetarian." —*Publishers Weekly*

$12.95 • Paper • ISBN 0-89594-053-1

Taste of the Tropics
Traditional and Innovative Cooking from the Pacific and Caribbean

By Jay Solomon

Part travelogue, part cookbook, with helpful hints and tasty tips for using tropical ingredients, this book is the next best thing to being there!

$10.95 • Paper • ISBN 0-89594-533-9

Traveling Jamaica with Knife, Fork & Spoon

By Robb Walsh and Jay McCarthy

Take an adventurous trip across the island of Jamaica with 140 recipes and dozens of colorful characters along the way.

$16.95 • Paper • ISBN 0-89594-698-X

To receive a current catalog from The Crossing Press
please call toll-free,
800-777-1048.
Visit our Web site on the Internet: www. crossingpress.com